JOE AVERAGE BROTHER

"A Collection of Poems And Short Stories"

PAUL WILSON

Published And Distributed By
Professional Publishing House
1425 W. Manchester Ave. Ste. B
Los Angeles, California 90047
323-750-3592
Email: professionalpublishinghouse@yahoo.com
www.Professionalpublishinghouse.com

Cover design: Jessica Tilles/TWASolutions.com
First Printing: April 2015
978-0-9861557-1-0
10987654321

ACKNOWLEDGEMENTS & DEDICATIONS

First, I must acknowledge my parents, Rogers Wilson, Sr. and Joan Estella Wilson. May they both rest in peace. Mad props go out to Dr. Rosie Milligan, Founder and Executive Director of Black Writers on Tour. She has, for at least two decades, encouraged me to write my book.

To my friends at Super Shuttle, dispatcher Eddie Smith, drivers Neva Fambrough and Michael Draffen. Also to Lennard Davis, Ph.D., for his stories about being at San Jose State University during the days of Olympians Lee Evans, Ronnie Ray Smith, Tommie Smith and John Carlos. May Lennard rest in peace.

To my friends in the activist community, starting with Ms. Georgiana Williams. Thank you for standing up for your son, Damien. To Mollie Bell, who introduced me to that early-morning radio talk show, "Front Page" on Radio-free, 102.3 KJLH. This station is owned by Stevie Wonder. Also to Mary Randall, formerly known as "Mary of Paramount." I still think you are cute!

To my dear friend, Ms. Patience Taylor, who helped me through my times of hospitalization and homelessness. She believed in me when I was having difficulty believing in myself. Also to the staff of JWCH and the Salvation Army at the Bell Shelter. Special props go out to Pastor Moore, who I called "Mister Enthusiasm." He encouraged me to enter essay contests for Martin Luther King Day and President's Day in 2012.

To the staff of JWCH at the Weingart Center on Skid Row in Downtown Los Angeles. I still owe you guys that pizza party I promised you. Special props go out to Zen Austin (Zulu Alpha), for encouraging me to share my writing at the various spoken-word venues she told me about.

To Charles Williams, host of Freedom of Speech Thursdays at Sabor y Cultura Internet Café in Hollywood. To Lady Basco, host of Speakeasy Mondays at The Last Bookstore in Downtown Los Angeles. To the hosts and musicians of "Flight School" at the Industry Café in Culver City, where I met someone I spent ten years searching for.

To Ms. Gia Scott-Heron, daughter of my hero, the late, great Gil Scott-Heron. You are not bragging when you warn people that you are "Hot!" Whenever I need to cheer myself up, I watch that scene from the documentary, "Black Wax," where you are walking down the street with your father.

To Don Del Gado, Department of Veterans Affairs, who told me about the VRAP program. This information got me to attend Los Angeles Trade Technical College (LATTC). To Ray Lampano, Instructor, Computer Information Systems. His knowledge of African American history and culture still amazes me.

To my new friends at LATTC. Vanessa Van Wagner, a poet in her own right. Professors Freddie McClain, Lionel B. Coulter and Thurman Robinson. The fact that they like my writing tells me I might be on to something.

To Barbara Lewis, a fellow veteran who kept me focused when I lost sight of my goals. To Lauren Shy Smith "Princess Shy" and her daughter, Kai Imala-Zuri Smith, the "Princess in Training."

To Barbara Joas (don't EVEN ask me how to pronounce her last name!) I just know her as Barbara J, "Fearless Barbara".

To Ms. Alicia Randolph, librarian at the West Los Angeles Regional Branch of the Los Angeles Public Library. To Ms. Hope Anita Smith, whose "Wordshops" helped to develop my writing skills.

To Rhonda Yvette Dula, PhD, who took an interest in me before I knew that I might be interesting. And, to her little sister, Vernice Armour, "Flygirl", the first African American Female Marine Corps Helicopter Combat Pilot. She served two tours in Iraq. Vernice is now a motivational speaker and author of *Zero to Breakthrough*.

TABLE OF CONTENTS

Zulu Alpha

Pen to paper, late at night
Because I've got the urge to write!
Hearing this, you'll know it's time
That I get major help with rhyme!

1945 elevator
Tell the Weingart Center, "Later!"
Soon I will be out that door
Headed to the Last Bookstore.

Yo', contender, what you know?
To Speak easy, he won't go!
I catch the bus anyway
As this might still be a good day!

Hit the bookstore right at eight
S.R.O. because I'm late.
At the door, I'm told by spirit,
"Zen is AWOL?" I can't hear it!
Bu I still go on inside.
Since I'm here, I'll take the ride!

Irish Nigel is on deck,
Listen to him, what the heck?
Has this thing for chocolate sisters,
And once again, my brain blisters.
He caught one near Inglewood,
Now, what he know about "the hood?"

Homies, check out his attire,
Red don't go there, blue's required.
Nigel's sweatin', gonna wig,
So he does an Irish jig!

Homies do not kick his ass,
They grant him a "ghetto pass."
Nigel now can do his thing.
In honor of Rodney King.

Jeff the Redd comes up on stage,
Don't drop science, turn the page.
He tells us a music story,
All about the three-chord glory.
Yo, hip hoppers, please take note,
His "Wild Thing" ain't by Tone Loc!

A red-headed brother sings about,
A flick he watched while half passed out.
Then he does the Spanish boogie,
No Van McCoy, or oogie, oogie.

Another guy says, "Life's a bitch,"
Because just like us, he ain't rich!
At 2200, I receive
A trump card from Speakeasy's sleeve.

"Happy Girl" was standing there,
I did not know she had blue hair!
She gets props, I cannot diss,
Her act I'm glad I did not miss!

She did not sing a dancing tune,

But her song took me to the Moon!
Having heard her do her thing,
I know Happy Girl can sing!

"Zulu Alpha, where are you?
I came here to hear your crew.
Others may know you as Zen,
When will I see you again?"

Because of you, I took the time,
To try my hand at writing rhyme.
You told me about this place,
Open mike in cyberspace.

Having had to risk the pain,
Helped to exercise my brain!

Anti-"Meow" Man

This is the story about a gay boy I heard
At the Last Bookstore. His performance was
A response to a guy the previous week
Who expressed his love for that most delicate
And wonderful aspect of the female anatomy.

After receiving much opposition from two
Females whom I have mad respect for, I decided
To curtail my gratuitous use of the p-word.
This is the edited version; wanna hear it?
Here it go.

Ooh, bop, shaboo, ooh, bop, shabam.
There goes the Ain't "Meow" Man!
He ain't had Kat since Kat had him,
Don't blame me if he don't like trim.

When he described his situation,
He did not hide his orientation.
His ideal man was tall, black and firm,
His description made some sisters squirm!

Was this an ad or maybe a promo?
He straight up said, "I'm a homo!"
This piece was not meant to offend,
I called it as I heard it, friend.

During Anti-"Meow" Man's performance,
The sound man at the Last Bookstore

Played the beginning of Gil Scott-Heron's
Very first album, "Small Talk at 125th and
Lennox." If you know that album, you'll
know where I'm from on that.

I was more inclined to think about tracks
Number six and eight from the Funkadelic
Album, "America Eats Its Young." Take into
Consideration that when those albums were
Released, certain words and terms weren't
Known to be offensive. They are now.
I hope I didn't step on anybody's toes
This was just my reaction to his reaction.

I actually have sympathy for the LGBT

Community. My parents (Mom in particular)
taught me to speak "proper English." If you
 are a young brother in the hood and you talk
like that, your sexual orientation will get challenged
on a regular basis. Polite people would say you had
"affected speech." Rude people will spread rumors
About your being gay even though they don't know
Diddly-squat about you!

There was one guy who accused me of being
Gay. I shut him up with a quickness! I told him,
"I am proud to inform you that your little sister is no
longer a virgin." Maybe you should get ready to be an uncle.
Considering that your name is Thomas, what would that make you?

To: Nicety, From a Former Horndog

For hardcore rap, go to Ice-T,
For sensuous rhyme, call Nicety.
I read books about Easy Rawlins,
Were you influenced by Bootsy Collins?
Well, I don't know, but maybe,
So, "Yabba dabba doozie, baby!"

Nicety came within my reach
In Hollywood, at Freedom of Speech,
Introduced by C-Will,
Her looks gave me one big thrill!
Now, it's not polite for me to stare,
But I'm turned on by her red hair!

I'll dodge the flak when this comes out,
For the kind of girl Mixalot raps about,
Before you tell me, "Not so fast,"
Baby got back and she can put 'em on the glass!
Moves so smooth, body so ample,
She's the lady I wanna sample!

Lemme work this rhyme, I'm on a roll
I'm thinkin' about Kindred, the Family Soul,
We could fit like hand in glove,
If only you would surrender to love.
You woke me up, I've got that pep,
Time for me to "glide, step!"
Am I real? Well, I could be,

Right now this is a fantasy.
A romantic picnic, a secluded park,
Take you on a long walk after dark,
And if I may be so bold,
Here's a blanket so coochie don't catch a cold!

Sailing on a moonlit lake,
Serve you filet mignon steak,
Champagne for you, a gleam in my eye,
You take me on a natural high!
Let's get busy, I can't wait,
Your curves would make a gay boy straight!

Please don't cop an attitude,
I want you in a sexy mood.
You make me woozy, weak in the knees,

Got me talkin' 'bout the birds and the bees.
We could kick it 'til the break of dawn,
Bonita Applebum, you gotta put me on!

There are important things that matter,
What's on my mind? "Hot Sex on a Platter!"
I close the door, to avoid the nosey,
And remember wisdom from Doctor Rosie,
Her words make sense; I must rewind, "Stroke the mind before the
behind!"

Some diss my bald head, tryin' to be mean,
But it's just a solar panel on a sex machine!
Your mental is excellin' let me make this plain,
If I could do it safely, I would lick your brain!
The Tribe said it best, and it's not that odd,

"Oh, my God, yes, oh, my God."

I'm out there in orbit, for what it's worth,
Hit my retro rockets to come down to earth!
Beauty and talent rolled into one,
Dag, she might already be with someone!
Can't afford the romance the way I wanna, G,
Time for me to sit down and face reality!

Nicety told me she was gonna host a poetry slam,
Threw a couple rhymes together, wanna try to jam!
Called her so the details we could discuss,
Forgot to tell her that I had to ride the bus!
Her function starts at seven, I got there at eight,
Should I tell her that MTA was running late?

When I got there both the party and the ladies were fine,
Only problem was the last bus left her place at nine,
I just sat there with my head in my lap,
Time ran out before I even got a chance to rap!
That's what I get for frontin' like I was fly,
I'm just Joe Average Brother, a regular guy!

Ava Small: U.S.A.F.

When I was in the Air Force, I had a friend with whom I had gone through Officer Training School. Her name was Second Lieutenant Ava Small. We were stationed together at Mather Air Force Base in Sacramento, California.

Ava was a very proper southern sister, straight outta Valdosta, Georgia. One day, her father called to tell her he was coming to visit her. As there were no direct flights from Valdosta to Sacramento, he had to drive to Atlanta and fly to San Francisco.

Ava asked me to ride with her to San Francisco to pick up her father. While I was honored that she asked me, I had to know why? Her beauty and southern hospitality would make most of the guys on base want to be her travelling companion.

"You're from California, aren't you?" she asked.

"Yes, but I'm from Los Angeles. That's a good four hundred miles south of Sacramento."

"Haven't you been to San Francisco before?"

"Maybe three or four times in my lifetime."

"I've never been there before. Since you're in navigator school, you could look at the maps and make sure I'm going the right way."

I wasn't gonna turn her down; I just wanted to see her sweat. She did everything else so well.

Anyhow, we made it to San Francisco three hours ahead of her father's scheduled arrival time. Ava now wanted to tour the city. Where could I take her and get back to the airport in time for her father's flight?

I decided on the Marina. We could drive up Van Ness Avenue. When we got to the top of the hill, we could look down and see Fisherman's Wharf.

While waiting at the light, we saw something that startled Ava's Southern sensibilities. Two guys were crossing the street, hand in hand. They both wore poorly applied makeup, false eyelashes, micro-mini skirts and six-inch stiletto heels. It was obvious that they were both guys as their Adam's Apples and five o'clock shadows were prominent. Ava, on the verge of hysteria, started pointing and screaming.

"What's wrong with those two guys? Don't they have any decency? Why are they doing this in broad daylight?"

I tried to calm Ava down, while, at the same time, I avoided bursting into laughter.

"Ava, you're a Southern lady. You know it's not polite to point. Welcome to California, in general, and San Francisco. in particular. They live here; you're the one visiting. Rest assured, if they are out in public like this, they definitely can fight. Most likely, I could handle one without much difficulty, but two? Both wearing stiletto heels--I could wind up singing higher than Michael Jackson!"

As soon as we found a safe place to make a U-turn, we quickly exited the Marina area and made a bee line to the airport. I have said on many occasions, how Los Angeles and Orange County are two entirely different worlds. If that is the case, then San Francisco is a different planet altogether!

We got to the terminal ten minutes before her father's flight landed. Standing next to me was a hippie, casually smoking a joint, as if it was only a cigarette. Ten feet from us was an Airport Police Officer. I decided to get away from the hippie so the cop wouldn't accuse me of having sold the joint to the hippie.

They didn't call it racial profiling back then, but it still worked the same. The Black man would get blamed for the white man's crime.

Notes on the
Leimert Park Village Book Fair

On June 30, 2012, I had another opportunity to get out in the community. I attended the Sixth Annual Leimert Park Village Book Fair. Honestly, this is the first time I actually paid attention to it. I normally focus my energy towards Dr. Rosie Milligan's Black Writer's on Tour event. This year I decided to investigate what other people are doing to promote literacy in the Black community.

The book fair had as one of several sponsors, radio station KJLH. Dominique Di Prima, host of the early morning talk show "Front Page," made sure her listeners were well-aware of the event.

Quite possibly, the one singular event that might have divided the forces of the *Front Page* family was the home going service of Rodney G. King. Prior to his death, Mr. King had been scheduled to be interviewed by Earl Ofari Hutchinson at the book fair. Rodney's book, *The Riot Within*, had just been released. Many went to honor "the accidental hero," as opinionated columnist Jasmyne A. Cannick described him.

Actress, singer, and self-proclaimed "Diva," Sheryl Lee Ralph, was one of many celebrities present at the book fair. Among others were the poets Sonia Sanchez and Amiri Baraka. I jokingly refer to Baraka as "The poet formerly known as Leroi Jones." He also happens to be Dominique Di Prima's father.

I think I actually saw Ms. Di Prima. I am not certain, as I have only seen her once before in person. Many *Front Page* family members recognize each other by their voices. The lady whom I suspect was Dominique was light-skinded (I speak ebonics on purpose!), petite, and was dragging a young boy with her. The boy appeared to be about seven years of age. The lady was wearing faded jeans and a t-shirt, which read "Front Page Team." I didn't attempt to speak to her as she appeared to have her hands full with the young man, whom I assume was her son.

I came to Leimert Park to look for several people in particular. One was the actress, Karen Malina-White. I feel I owe that sister an apology for something I did back in 1994. I heard she was going to be at the book fair; however, I was not successful in finding her. I was also looking for the author, Jervey Tervalon. I felt the *Front Page* family owed him an apology, and I was prepared to offer him one on our behalf. I figured since he is an author that he might actually show up. No joy on spotting him either. When my book is published, both apologies will be in it and I will attempt to locate and send each of them a copy.

There were other celebrities I had better luck in finding. One of them was Dr. Rosie Milligan, who is one of my "Sheroes." I have heard people describe her as the "Modern Day Harriet Tubman." I think of her more like Sojourner Truth. Doctor Rosie is a tall woman. She travels far and wide, speaking truth to power. In a way, I guess she is like Mrs. Tubman, as she is leading African-Americans to freedom through economic empowerment and literacy.

Los Angeles County Supervisor, Mark Ridley-Thomas, was another celebrity I was able to find. We were able to briefly recall our days as students at Manual Arts High School. Mark was our Senior Class President. We also attended a camp together in 1971. I mentioned him in my upcoming book. I also told him about my concept of "Martin Luther King's Greatest Hits." Mark agreed that we shouldn't limit ourselves to his "I have a Dream," and "I've Been to the Mountain Top," speeches. Dr. King spoke on so many other important issues.

There were so many interesting presentations going on simultaneously that I almost missed the opportunity to meet Dr. Firpo Carr. He was speaking about his book, *Germany's Black Holocaust: 1890-1945*. Dr. Carr confirmed that what Hitler did to the Jews during World War II was first done to Africans by Kaiser Wilhelm in the 1890s. I was able to answer Firpo's question about Rocket Scientist Werner Von Braun. His work was instrumental in enabling America to win the "Space Race" against the Soviet Union, putting a man on the Moon in 1969. This was the same guy who designed the V-2 Rocket that terrorized Great Britain during the latter stages of World War II.

The United States Office of Strategic Services (OSS) brought Von Braun and other German Rocket Scientists to America during Operation Paper Clip. I wouldn't be surprised if Dr. Firpo knew how Reinhard Gehlen was a German General one day, and became an American General the next!

I especially wanted to know if Firpo Carr graduated from Locke High School in 1972. It turned out that he attended both Jordan and Locke High Schools, but graduated from Chaffey High School in Ontario. I attended U.C. Irvine with several 1972 and 1973 graduates of David Starr Jordan High School in L.A. (Not to be confused with Long Beach Jordan). I was also involved in an Upward Bound program at Los Angeles City College during the summers of 1969, '70, '71 & '72, with students from Alain Leroy Locke High School.

Joe Average Brother Visits Awkward Black Girl

Awkward people, awkward times,
Rappers slingin' awkward rhymes.
Roaming through this awkward world,
I go check out "Awkward Black Girl."

Is she awkward, by any chance,
because home girl cannot dance?
Does she work in awkward occupations?
Is she stuck in awkward situations?

I went to Exposition Park,
to check her out after dark.
I got there late, the joint was packed,
I had to sit way in the back.

All I knew about her hype,
was what I read in print or type.
I can't afford, at least not yet,
to surf the Web or Internet.

A thought I had from one episode,
Was, "Did they change the Ghetto Code?"
I don't think I'm that damn slow,
but dot dot, dit dit, dot dot, dash,
I'm damned if I know.

Before I get too unhip,
Let me vibe on the positive tip.

I saw nothing about drugs.
Brothers weren't portrayed as thugs.
It wasn't like they were all saints.
Sister did have some complaints.

Her Ex-boyfriend's a straight-up flake,
Even his sincere moves were fake!
He left her in a funky mood,
Then came back with an attitude.
The second time he was outta there,
Because she cut off all her hair!

"Awkward" makes his fact official,
As a people, we're superficial!
Home girl took her second strike,
When she stepped to another guy she liked.

At the party things were lookin' fly,
when she acquired her target guy.
Then his lady made it crystal clear,
to her man, "Awkward" bett' not get near!
Home girl starts to consider others,
Does this mean she is done with brothers?

"Awkward" took some bad advice.
On the one move, she should think twice!
To me, it just do not seem right,
To date someone just because they're White.

In her departure from dating a brother,
they didn't know much about each other.
He thought it would be all good,
if they went out to eat soul food.

The venue he chose was not that dizzy,
to the Marina to visit Aunt Kizzy.

The stares they got would make one quiver,
If eyes were knives, they'd be chopped liver!
To this reaction, don't be scared,
I think they should have been prepared.

The brothers who would give her fits,
are usually big hypocrites!
It would really rock their worlds,
if you caught them with their White girls!
For now, that's all I have to say,
I'll save the rest for another day!

Big Chicken Dinner? Not!

—⊷∈⊷—

While I was stationed at Nellis Air Force Base in Las Vegas, Nevada, I became a Squadron Section Commander; I carried "G Series" orders. This meant I could perform command functions, in lieu of my squadron commander. I represented my enlisted troops during their drug and alcohol rehab counseling sessions.

What I am most proud of was that I was able to save a Black Master Sergeant from receiving a Bad Conduct Discharge (BCD). This discharge was suggested by a White Clinical Psychologist, who happened to be a Lieutenant Colonel. The Master Sergeant in question was at the NCO Club one night when he encountered some friends he had served with in Vietnam. All of a sudden it was "Old Home Week" for him. During his reunion, he stayed at the club longer and consumed more liquor than he had intended.

Once he left the NCO Club, our Master Sergeant was pulled over by base Security Police for driving under the influence (DUI), then he was placed under arrest. Present at his counseling session were a Social Actions Officer (a Black Captain and former Security Police Officer), a Chaplain (a Black Major), and a Psychologist (the White Lieutenant Colonel), and me (a lowly First Lieutenant.)

For some strange reason, the Psychologist thought he was in charge of this counseling session. I wonder why? Both the Social Actions Officer and the Chaplain knew I had G-Series orders. They deferred to my recommendations on how to proceed in this case.

Our Master Sergeant, who received endorsements on his Airman Performance Reports (APR's) from flag-ranked officers (Generals and Admirals), was a highly-decorated troop. Upon checking his record, this was the first time he had ever been in any kind of trouble.

Apparently, this meant nothing to Mister Psychologist. He strongly suggested I fine, bust, and discharge the Master Sergeant. This conversation should not have been held in front of the Master Sergeant. Since the Psychologist initiated this exchange, I had no intention of backing down. In front of the Lieutenant Colonel, I told the Master Sergeant what was going to happen to him.

"Sergeant, since this is your first offense, you are going to receive a suspended bust. This means that while you will still wear the stripes and perform the duties of a Master Sergeant, you will receive the pay of a Technical Sergeant (one step lower in rank). This situation will occur for a period of six months. If you perform your duties in the exemplary manner, which was your norm prior to this incident, you will be restored to your regular pay grade. If, however, you are involved in another similar incident, further action may be considered against you, up to and possibly including, an Other Than Honorable Discharge."

The Psychologist strongly objected to my decision. Somehow, he didn't realize this was not a "Suggestion" on my part. This was a "Done Deal" for the Master Sergeant. The Psychologist felt I should confer with my commanding officer before making such a "Hasty and Ill-advised Decision." Since he out-ranked me, I allowed him to fire the first "Shot." Now, it was time for my "counter measures."

"Lieutenant Colonel, (I had no intention of calling him "Sir"), which commanding officer are you referring to? My acting commanding officer is a First Lieutenant as am I. Not only do I outrank him by three months, but I have two years more experience in performing command functions. While I defer to his experience in keeping our aircraft flying, he defers to mine in dealing with administrative matters, of which this is one. Since you question my authority, I will grant you the honor of contacting my superior officer so that you can personally express your misgivings about my decision making abilities.

"My Lieutenant Colonel is currently on Temporary Duty (TDY) in Germany with two-thirds of the 474th Tactical Fighter Wing. Here is the Autovon Number where you can reach him. It is

presently 0300 hours there. Good luck in convincing him why I should discharge the man who is directly responsible for keeping our brand-new, perfectly good F-16's from falling out of the sky when we were having problems with their Emergency Power Units (EPU's) during the summer of 1981."

The Psychologist attempted to suggest that this must be a "Black Thing" since he was the only White person in the room.

In return, I informed him of how the vast majority of the pilots, who depended on the sergeant's technical expertise, were White. The officers who endorsed his APR's were White, especially the flag officer whose name was of Slavic (Eastern European) origin. So how could this be a "Black Thing?" No, I countered, it was the right thing to do. I also reminded the Psychologist that he was there in an advisory capacity only. My position superseded his rank in this manner. He had walked into this trap of his own accord. I was just the guy who happened to snare him!

I felt good taking a stand as a Black man, and having the authority to do it. It was a lesson I would never forget.

Fearless Barbara

Gotta get to Barbara J's,
Check out her Fearless Fridays.
For singing, she's a natural choice,
And spoken word, she's got that voice!

I wonder who her mentors are,
I predict she will go far.
Verbally unafraid to get it on.
She gives tribute to young Trayvon.

What did Sister learn in school?
Home girl is nobody's fool!
Barbara J can handle stress.
Therefore, with her please don't mess!

Did Sister Barbara get so wise,
by shutting down knuckle-headed guys?
Basically, she's kind to others,
But one night she got rough on the brothers!

I'd like to sit with her awhile,
to gaze upon her lovely smile!
She lets no one get on her nerves.
On top of that she's got the curves!

It's not as if I were a crook.
I'm single and straight, I'm gonna look!
In fact, I will go to great pains,
seeking beautiful sisters with brains!

I'd like to help spread unity,
through our diverse community!
Check out what Brother C-Will did.
one summer, he worked with Project GRYD

Or like Brother Sativa Green,
who peeped the secret society scene!
Proving that some conspiracies,
are scandals and not just theories!

I liked Rhys Langston and his views,
as he gave props to Langston Hughes.
You develop the skills, now acquire the knowledge,
while you're at that Connecticut College.
Stretch that envelope as you push it.
Heed Jessie's warning, "Stay out the Bushes!"

Lady Basco at the Last Bookstore,
showed me that I could do so much more.
There are some things that she can say,
with which I can't dream of getting away!
But I can stop being such a sap,
I can get up and bust a cap!

Because of you, my mental grows,
For all my new Heroes and Sheroes,
My time is short, but I'm not done,
I just can't mention everyone.
If I didn't shout you out, don't feel excluded,
But, in conclusion, I have concluded!

Zen Austin/Jeff Baldinger/Racial Ambiguity

Let me Start This Piece Off by Saying How Much I like going to Speakeasy Mondays at the Last Bookstore. I stopped coming for a while, for reasons I had to reconsider. Upon returning to the stage, Lady Basco welcomed me back, though. I look at Speakeasy Mondays as sort of a laboratory for performance artists.

My "Zulu Alpha" poem is based on my observations of the performers at the Last Bookstore on May 28, 2012. That was the first poem I've written since junior high school and the first rap I've ever performed on stage. It started out as a letter to a lady named Zen Austin. I guess I have to consider her my muse. When I told her I was writing a book, she suggested I read some of it at the Last Bookstore and a Sabor Y Cultura Internet Café.

Zen Austin (Zulu Alpha) was part of a band called "The GYFT." She sings, plays guitar, and does spoken word readings. I would write her a letter after seeing her perform. Sometimes, I would write her after thinking about something she and I discussed. This once caused me to hand her three letters at the same time! Zen was my first source of intellectual stimulation when I became a client of the Weingart Center. She provided a banquet for this starving brother!

I have a penchant for intelligent sisters. I also love to see sisters smile. Add to this the fact that she was strikingly attractive and musically gifted and you see that I was dealing with a quadruple threat!

"Comedian Jeff Baldinger is another source of material for me. I've heard him talk about science, music and racial ambiguity. Jeff has red hair, so I referred to him as "Jeff the Redd." In my "Zulu Alpha" rap/poem. I also call him Jeffrey Heisenberg. I used "Heisenberg," due to my "uncertainty" about his actual last name. This was a "compensator" until I could actually learn what his last name was. Unless you are a serious fan of "Star Trek," you might not have a clue as to the inside jokes I'm making here. That's why I'm not even going to talk about the Jeffries tubes that the engineering staff used to traverse between critical parts of the Starship Enterprise.

Recently, Jeff talked about how Black people have come up to him to inquire if he himself was African-American; I, for one, can understand this. In college I had a roommate named Leslie Styles. He was a light-skinded brother from San Diego. Leslie was about the same height as Jeff and had red hair. If they stood side by side, you would think they were related.

One day when my car wouldn't start, Mr. Styles gave me a ride to work. One of my Filipino co-workers asked who that White guy was who dropped me off. When I told him that was my roommate, and that he was Black, my co-worker shouted, "Noooo!"

Also while in college, I met a girl named Kathy Brooks. She was a Jewish girl from Southern Ohio. Kathy wore her hair in a style I've heard referred to as a "Jewfro." I told her that my mother was from Toledo, Ohio and that her maiden name was Brooks. I suggested that Kathy and I could possibly be related. Her White friends who were listening to this conversation started looking at her funny. Kathy starts rubbing her arm and says, "Well, I don't really think so, do you?"

I proceeded to tell her how several members of my mother's family were light enough to pass for White and left Toledo for Southern Ohio in order to do so. All of a sudden, Kathy no longer wanted to talk to me.

A lot of the Black students made a "Project" out of Kathy Brooks. We would go out of our way to speak to her. We would say things like, "Good morning, Kathy," "How you doin', Sister?" and "We're having a BSU meeting tonight. See you there."

She would make comments to her White friends like, "I seem to be popular among the Black students here," while laughing nervously. I even heard one White girl call her, "Peola," referring to the female lead from the movie, "Imitation of Life."

In one of Jeff Baldinger's routines, he makes reference to the Black Panthers. Here goes a related story for you. During the days of the

FBI's Counter Intelligence Program, (COINTELPRO) and "Operation Chaos" (no, we're not talking about Maxwell Smart's adversaries), UCLA Professor Angela Davis was on the run from Gay Edgar Hoover's boys (notice how I didn't say J. Edgar Hoover). She had legitimate concern to fear for her life (no-knocked on my brother Fred Hampton, bullet holes all over the place). Angela Davis surrendered to the FBI in 1970. She made sure she did so in a <u>very</u> public place. Ms. Davis was dressed conservatively in a dark, knee-length skirt, light colored blouse and had her hair pulled back. When I saw the pictures of her being "Perp Walked" in handcuffs, if I didn't know that was Angela Davis, I would have wondered if she were a sister or not. She looked like "Wonder Woman's" alter ego Diana Prince.

Then there is the interesting case of the late songstress Phoebe Snow (may she rest in peace). Back in 1988, I read an article about her in *USA Today*. She talked about how on many occasions after her concerts, she would get cornered in the ladies' room by a throng of sisters staring at her, trying to figure out if she was Black. We (black people) had reason to wonder. Ms. Snow had a loyal Black following. We flocked to her concerts in droves. Her voice was very soulful. She delivered her songs in the R&B tradition. Phoebe had Black back-up singers, for goodness sake!

During the first season of the *Cosby Show* spinoff, *A Different World*, Phoebe Snow sang the show's theme song. In the early 1990s, there was a situation comedy on Fox starring Matt Frewer. (us older folks remember him as "Max Headroom"). At the beginning of that show, Phoebe sings, "Standing on Shaky Ground." That song was originally performed by the Temptations! What did you expect Black people to think? Upon seeing her on album covers, on televisions, or in person, we still thought, "It's possible."

In that newspaper article, Phoebe Snow attempts to explain her physical appearance. "My father was a Moor. A Moor is a Spanish Jew."

"Takamuna! Wait a minute! I'm gonna have to find a dictionary and look up the definition of "Moor." Based on what I think I know, the

Moors were originally from Northern Africa. Many of them converted (or were "converted") to Islam during the Seventh Century A.D. In the year 711 the Moors, along with other Muslims, invaded Southwest Europe. This includes what is now Spain, Portugal and parts of Southern France. The countries of Morocco and Mauritania derive their names from the word "Moor."

I get the impression that "Moor" is a term used by people who classify themselves as "White" to describe people who they don't consider to be "White." Consider this: according to the historian, Runoko Rashidi, Beethoven was described as a "Blackamoor." Go figure!

Beware of the Boule'

-->====(o)

This particular piece will be for the edification of Stephen King, AKA Sativa Green. This will also be a tribute to researcher, political activist, and Freedom Fighter, the late, great Steve Cokely.

Brother Cokely grew up in Chicago, having attended Catholic school there. He went to Northern Illinois University on a baseball scholarship. He was always interested in the inner workings of political organizations, having gotten up close and personal with the Chicago political machine.

Cokely worked with the NAACP, Congressman Gus Savage and Mayor Harold Washington. He got my attention on May 5, 1988, when on ABC's *Nightline* program, Brother Cokely debated Republican Pat Buchanan. He shut Buchanan up!

He did the same thing on February 28, 1998 to conservative talk show, host Larry Elder, the self-proclaimed, "Sage of South Central." The topic of their debate was, "Is There Racism in Hollywood?"

Larry Elder attempted to argue that there was no racism in Hollywood. Cokely actually got Elder to admit that there was! Actress and Screen Actors Guild member, Ann Marie Johnson, put the icing on the cake when she made reference to the movie, "Krippendorf's Tribe," starring Richard Dreyfus. Ms. Johnson said that Black people would never get the green light to make a similar movie about Jewish people, but I digress.

Brother Cokely lectured about the secret societies in general and Black secret societies in particular. For example, the reason that Black Masons venerate Prince Hall is that he rescued the Charter that allowed them to set up their Masonic Chapters in America. This Charter was aboard the ship that was set ablaze in Boston Harbor during the Boston Tea Party.

Those of you who know about Black fraternities and sororities know about the, "Devine Nine." Did you know that there is one Black fraternity that is older than those? It is called Sigma Pi Phi, otherwise known as the Boule'. This secret society was founded in 1904 and was based on the tenets of Skull and Bones. That is the secret society at Yale that the Bushes belong to.

Only men can become Boule' members, they are called Archons. The wives are called Archausas. Their children are known as Archausen.

It turns out that I went to school with some Archausen. I don't wish to put them on blast since they never did anything against me.

Some famous Black men were Boule' members. W.E.B. DuBois organized the New York Chapter. Carter G. Woodson, the father of Negro History Week, quit the Boule' after they came out against Marcus Garvey. Alain Leroy Locke, author of "The New Negro" and major force in the Harlem Renaissance Movement was a Boule' member. He was also the first African-American Rhodes Scholar. A high school in Watts is named after him.

Many Black mayors of large American cities were Boule' members, so were certain sports figures (Arthur Ashe), gifted physicians (Dr. Ben Carson) and civil rights leaders (Martin Luther King, Jr.). In his "Drum Major" speech Dr. King talks about belonging to two fraternities, one of them was the Boule'.

So far, I have only found two books that even mention the Boule'. One is *Black Bourgeoisie* by noted Sociologist E. Franklin Frazier. The other is, *Our Kind of People* by law professor and prolific author, Lawrence Otis Graham. Radio talk show host, Carl Nelson interviewed Graham when his book was first published. Lawrence clowned Nelson for saying that his book was about the Black middle class. He specifically told Carl Nelson that his book was about the Black Upper Class.

Traditionally, Boule' members will not discuss anything about the Boule' with non-Boule' members. They will usually get up and leave the room. This is the same thing that happens when you try to discuss Skull and Bones with Skull and Bones members.

While I am not speaking against the organization as a whole, there are certain Boule' members who have done things to the detriment of African-Americans as a whole.

Because of the stance he took, Steve Cokely fell out with many of his fellow freedom fighters. He would offer this explanation: "When it comes to identifying the enemy, I have no friends."

Somewhere around 2003, while Carl Nelson was still host of "Front Page," comedian, political satirist, and health guru Dick Gregory debated Steve Cokely. While he didn't necessarily win the debate, Dick Gregory proceeded to clown Steve. This incident caused me to do the "Arsenio Hall", (things that make you go "Hmmm").

In January of 1988, Dick Gregory came to my Alma Mater, U.C. Irvine, to give the keynote address at the King Day celebration. He explained his theory concerning the unexpected recent death of Chicago Mayor Harold Washington. He said, "I-t could have been done with Binary Poisons." One of his aides could have handed the Mayor a document laced with one part of the poison one day. The next day, a different aide could hand the mayor another document laced with the other part of the poison. Each part of the poison by itself is inert, therefore, neither aide would suffer any ill effects. However, once both chemicals combine in your body, the target will fall over dead and it will look like a heart attack.

A few years after the Cokely – Gregory debate, I asked Dick Gregory if he ever discussed his theory about Harold Washington's death with Steve Cokely? He said, he never did. Hmmm!

"Millard Lowe Pregnant Mind"
13 July 2012

Time to pull another, "All Nighter." I've had my Munchies, two cans of "Pit Bull" and all sorts of ideas crashing my subliminal. So much that I don't know where to start, but here it goes anyway.

I'm gonna dedicate this session to a brother named Millard Lowe. I met Brother Lowe in November of 1984, while I was interviewing for a job as a Manager for Church's Fried Chicken. Millard had just returned from Jamaica after teaching there for thirteen years. He came to look after his ailing mother.

M. Lowe and I trained at Church's Master Merchant training store on Broadway and Gage Avenue in Los Angeles. This was during the time that the cartoon "Inspector Gadget" was popular. Our crew members called me "Inspector Gadget" and M. Lowe, "Chief Quimby." Whenever things at the store didn't go according to plan, I would tell Milllard, "Sorry about that, Chief."

When we completed our manager training course, Millard and I were assigned to different stores. Lowe worked at the store on Western Avenue and Imperial Highway. I was assigned to the store on Adams Boulevard and Central Avenue. On Sunday nights, after we completed our weekly reports, I would pick Millard up. We would proceed to the steakhouse that used to be on the southeast corner of Manchester and Western Avenues. We would discuss what happened at our respective stores and exchange ideas on how to make our stores run more efficiently.

In the same parking lot as our steakhouse was a Boy's (now Ralph's) Supermarket. Some of Boy's management team hung out at our steakhouse on Sunday nights also. We would acknowledge each other. "Hello Church's." "Hello Boy's." We all understood how wild and wooly it could be sometimes to run a store in "The Hood."

1985

⋆⟴

I can give you an example of how crazy things could get. In early 1985, I was Assistant Manager of the store on Adams and Central. One day, there was this large-built brother who was giving people in the area a hard time. We assumed he was high on PCP (Angel Dust). This guy was challenging guys to fight him and chasing little old ladies into the street.

Along comes this older brother wearing a *London Fog* trench coat and a *Tam 'O Shanter* (beret). He looked like he was either an artist, a musician, or a former Black Panther. Based on what I saw him do, I guess he had been a Panther back in the day. Now mind you. I am watching this episode unfold from the relative safety of being inside the store.

Apparently, our big built "dusted" friend must have challenged Mr. Beret to a fight. Mr. Beret was not intimidated by "Dust," but stood his ground instead. Dust was prancing around like he was Muhammad Ali. While advancing toward Dust, Mr. Beret was reaching into his coat pocket for a straight razor. Dust hit the ground when Mr. Beret hit him in the jaw. When Dust got up, he was bleeding like a stuck pig. He was now pleading for help from the same people he had been harassing earlier.

As a precautionary measure, Karen, our Store Manager and my boss, asked me to lock the doors to our store.

While I was doing that, Karen made this announcement: "Ladies and Gentlemen, you can either stay inside or leave our store, but we are locking our doors for the safety of those who wish to stay. We are also calling the police."

Next, Karen had me draw some hot peanut oil into a quart size pan from our #1 fryer. This was just in case our dusted friend managed to force his way into the store. Actually, Dust did attempt to gain entrance.

36

The whole front of our store was glass. When he couldn't get past our locked door, Dust took a trash can and cracked the glass in one of the doors. By this time, Dust had lost so much blood that he had no other choice but to sit down. I called 911 to report that a man who had tried to break into our store was now sitting in our parking lot bleeding profusely. I was hoping the paramedics would arrive before this guy bled out. However, the police showed up first.

The cops were trying to figure out how Dust got such a severe cut along the left side of his jaw. They thought it happened when he broke our glass door. I told them how this old guy popped him in the face with a straight razor. When they asked me where the old guy was, I told them how he hopped on a bus and split!

A similar incident occurred when Millard and I were at the store on Broadway and Gage. A guy with a guitar slung across his back came into the store, yelling like he was crazy. He was frightening our customers. "Guitar Man" pulled a combat knife on Millard when he was asked to leave the store. In three deft moves, M. Lowe disarmed Guitar Man and had him on the floor while telling him, "Give me the knife boy before you hurt your silly self with it!"

Upon returning to Los Angeles, Millard Lowe was the first person I felt comfortable confiding in about my experiences in college and the Air Force. As a teacher, Millard helped a lot of his students prepare for and get accepted to college. Before taking a position at a private school, M. Lowe spent the summer of 1985 involved in an Upward Bound Program at one of the Claremont Colleges.

By training, Millard was a Science Instructor. He also taught Black History, in general, and about the Civil Rights Movement, in particular. M. Lowe could give firsthand accounts about what happened in 1964 during "Freedom Summer" in Mississippi.

In addition, Millard was also a published poet. In Jamaica, he was known as "Pregnant Mind." My guess is that this meant he was always giving birth to new ideas.

Millard and I kept in touch after we both left Church's Fried Chicken. I took a management trainee position with Thrifty Drug

Stores (now known as Rite-Aid). Upon taking this job, I immediately received a $240.00 per month raise.

Millard Lowe was instrumental in helping me to maintain my sanity. Many of my friends whom I went to high school and college with were falling prey to the rock cocaine epidemic. "Rock" was the West Coast term for "Crack" cocaine. Eventually, crack was the term used for this form of cocaine across the country. While I smoked "Primo marijuana" and snorted "Pharmaceutical Grade" cocaine in college, I never smoked crack cocaine. I stopped using drugs in November 1979, three days before I joined the United States Air Force. I felt if I got the chance to fly, I would let that be my "High."

Blast for VLM (try not to use the P word)

Not caveat emptor, but caveat taster
You want us to keep your secrets?
You told us your secret while streaming <u>Live</u>!
You put yourself on blast, no Jive!

On this topic you should be discreet
Don't try to taste every Katt you meet!
If you advertise being a meow connoisseur
Stray Katz will beat a path to your door!

Back at the man cave / testosterone town
You'll be the subject of a serious clown!
No need to suffer such comedic strife
Concerning what should be your personal life!

Many guys who would make fun of you
Won't admit that they do it too!
If you accuse them, well golly gee whiz!
They'll say that it is none of your biz!

I wonder if this is your way
Of getting Mr. Richard a chance to play?
Is this the method you have found
For Richard to visit Jane's playground?

How do you create the situation
For Jane to come to your play station?

If you give Ms. Jane a lick
Will she work with your joystick?

Don't be the victim of male bashing,
First chance you get, give Jane a tongue lashing,
Making her experience one that's grand
Gets Richard invited to Loveland!

Don't be so rough, but start off gentle
For Richard it's physical, for Jane it's mental,
Dr. Rosie's wisdom, you must rewind,
"Stroke the mind before the behind!"

Yeeee, HA!
Don't fall victim to your pride
If Jane requests a moustache ride.
She is the star of your show
Call this the midnight rodeo!

Make sure that you rock her world
You can say "Ride "Em Cowgirl!"
Tell the truth, no time for lies,
Because you know you like her thighs!

You'll know you have won the day
When she screams, "Yipee Kai Yay!"
Once you master this technique,
Try not to become a freak.

Lady Basco, I Got Your Back

I consider myself pretty nervy at times. Once upon a time, I was downright arrogant. When I was nineteen years old, I thought I was bulletproof. Fortunately for me, nobody ever tested that theory!

In my yet to be published book, I have a chapter about the early morning talk show called "Front Page." It airs Monday through Friday from 4:30 to 6:00 A.M. on Radio Free, 102.3, KJLH. This station is owned by Stevie Wonder.

I lay out a set of guidelines or rules of etiquette for callers to the talk shows. If these guidelines were followed, more useful information could be disseminated and less superfluous nonsense would have to be tolerated by the listening audience.

Unfortunately, too many callers are more interested in hearing themselves speak than they are about that particular day's topic or guest. Some folks try to tell their life story, irrespective of the subject at hand.

Others insist on making a grand announcement every time they call in. We, the *Front Page* family already know who you are, just by your voice alone. "Get to the freaky-deaky point!"

Still other callers ramble and don't have a definitive statement to make or question to pose to the guest or host. This causes host Dominique Di Prima to go into her, "Time to Land the Plane," speech which wastes even more time! It would help if these callers would organize their thoughts and write them down before calling in.

This is the reason that when Lady Basco welcomes me to the stage, I bring my notebook with me. I came up without it once and proceeded to make a complete idiot of myself.

I challenge my fellow Front Page family members to The Last Bookstore so they can speak their piece, live and in person. There are a few things you should know before you try it, however.

You have five minutes to do your thing, be it playing music, singing, dancing, poetry, comedy, rapping or whatever it is that you do. Please get it in during your allotted five minutes.

We practice the "Dirty Thirty" rule here. The first thirty acts to sign up are guaranteed their time to shine. This is the reason we put the needle to the record at 8 o'clock sharp! If there's time left after those thirty acts, maybe we can have a jam session until we all have to pack up and leave at 11:00 p.m.

Speakeasy Mondays at the Last Bookstore is a very popular venue! If you wish to perform, sign-up starts at 7:45 p.m., I suggest you get here somewhat earlier than that. I have to wait in line to sign-up too, crutches and all!

The policy here is, "You Shine, I Shine. Please give those on stage the respect and courtesy that you would want when it is your turn to shine."

Lady Basco, I commend you for the work you do for Speakeasy Mondays. It is clearly obvious that there are other things that you could be and are doing in addition to this. If I were to publish a dictionary, your picture would appear alongside the definition of, "Multitasking."

The Friend Zone

The following page was inspired by the poet, "Ideas." The brother definitely has plenty of those! Ideas talked about how a guy might have a romantic interest in a particular female, only to find out that the lady considers him to be a friend.

This takes me back to a routine Chris Rock did. He talked about how the female friends most guys have are only women who he has yet to "Get With!" Think about it, fellas. How many times have you been the perfect gentleman to that one special someone, listened to her rants, helped her solve her problems, and basically just "Been There for Her!" You think it's finally time to let her know how you really feel about her. You are basically bearing your soul to her.

I don't know about you guys, but for me it happens like this: I am cautiously approaching the edge of, "Commitment Cliff." As I am telling her how I feel, cupid hasn't shot me with his bow and arrow. It's more like Zeus struck me with one of his lightning bolts, thus knocking me off the aforementioned cliff. When she gives you her response, it's not her voice you're hearing, but that of Rod Serling announcing, "You have entered the Friend Zone." Oh no, not again!

For the last six months you've been cultivating this, "Special Relationship." You think you are on the right track when she starts looking for you instead of the other way around. She tells you about how the last five guys she dated did her dirty. You strive not to be like those, "Dogs." You and the lady in question seem to be an item, especially to those women you've been looking at, but not trying to talk to. When she tells you how she feels, you try to maintain that air of confidence and bravado, but deep inside you want to run and hide! The Smokey Robinson tune, "Tears of a Clown," is usually playing in my head when this happens to me.

Now comes the time to consider inappropriate "Parting Shots." Some you only think about, others actually slip out. To the girl you thought was "The One," some of these lines come to mind:

"I didn't mind being your friend on the way to being your man."

"Sorry, but I have enough female friends whom I don't fool around with. Those positions have already been filled."

You have decided to check out the ladies who have been checking you out while you were playing," Mister Goody Good." You plan to get your mack on, only to realize that your mack muscles have atrophied due to lack of use. That happens when you practice being honest instead.

Me: Hi, Linda, I've been thinking about you. How about we do lunch so I can tell you a few things?

Linda: That sounds nice, but what about Debbie? I thought you two were pretty close.

Me: Think about it, Linda. If I had it like that with Debbie, why would I even be talking to you?

The art of macking involves emotion, not logic. Once you introduce logic, you automatically break any spell you might have been trying to cast.

Sister Janice

⊷═◉

For those of you who are computer savvy, I am requesting your assistance. I need to find out whatever happened to a sister named Janice Cobb. She was a poetess. Perhaps "Spoken Word Artist" would be the more appropriate term today.

She wrote a book called *Six Thousand, Five Hundred, Eighty-Eight Yesterdays*. If you divide that number by 366, you come up with approximately eighteen years. I met Sister Janice in the Spring of 1973. She was a senior at the University of San Francisco when I was a freshman at U.C. Irvine.

I was taking a class called, "Introduction to Black Culture," taught by then graduate student, Willie Mae Coleman. Ms. Coleman invited Janice to speak to our class.

I'm not sure how much hair Janice Cobb had; she might have been one of those "TWA" girls. TWA stands for "Teeny Weeny Afro." She wore an earring in her nose when doing such a thing was a novelty. Sister Janice wore ankle-length skirts when other women were wearing hot pants and micro mini-skirts.

She talked about the static she would get from the other students, especially from the brothers. The following is what I remember from her poem about her attire.

...and the brother said, "I sure wish you would wear some shorter skirts so I could talk some sweet shit to you."

And the sister replied, "Brother, if I have to raise my skirt just to hear some of your divine rap, I might as well drop my drawers and hear your whole conversation! Is that the price we have to pay for communication?"

Kim, the Comedian

It's only my opinion, that much is true
But I have a good opinion of you!
I'm so happy you don't exist
In the world of gay Jewish Scientologists!

You look good! And you have knowledge
Where were you when I was in college?
Together, we could have worked a business plan
'Cause back then I was the weed man!

Yeah, back in the day I sold the smoke
I had it going on, I wasn't no joke!
Financial aid was low, so I had no choice
'Cause I couldn't make cash with my singing voice!

And I sure didn't get by on my good looks
Had to spend heavy ducketts on tuition and books!
The recession made jobs hard to come by
So I got busy as "Connection Guy!"

I didn't squander all the money I made
Bodyguards and distributors all got paid,
I modestly furnished my apartment
And stayed three months ahead on my rent!

Drove a Volkswagen Bug, not trying to act rich
'Cause you never know who might wanna snitch!

Joe Average Brother

Didn't always roll strapped, but I had firepower,
I had lookouts I paid by the hour!

I began my endeavor as a sophomore
With a kilo of commercial that I did score!
Sifted out all the stems and collected the seed
And I sold my ounces with efficiency and speed!

To the Freshman class, I did sell
They became my loyal clientele!
Ounce by ounce, sold five keys in two weeks
And happened to identify a couple of freaks!

Banked some of my profit, fifteen percent,
Re-invested the rest and off I went!
But again I ask, "Kim where were you?"
When I think of all the nice things we could do!

I am not the type of brother who talks much trash
I would let you sample primo from my home grown stash!
When the munchies struck and it was time to eat
I would prepare a culinary treat!

Have a candlelight dinner, where we could flirt,
After dinner, could I have you for dessert?
Surviving rounds one, two, three, and four
We would be too tired to make that breakfast score!

To make it up to you,
so that you don't think I'm shady,
I would throw a banquet,
catered by the School Lunch Lady!
Then I'd take you shopping, you could buy a gown,

Designed by the new mob wife in town!
Don't get jealous, please, baby, please,
When she clicks her heels, she's got sexy knees!

Let's stay away from Dike Juice
She's so full of venom,
She's responsible for liberating
All my other women!

Nothing but a wild woman, causing panic
So let's hook her up with Jasmyne Cannick!
They could work together, steady on the case
Jasmyne's a reporter who stays in your face!

When looking for the answers,
Her search won't cease,
She's the reason that we know
What happened to Mitrice?

This is the reason
That me and you,
Will not be going out
To dinner in Malibu!

While I like having fun,
I'm allergic to drama,
That's why we won't hang out
With Rednecks for Obama!

Only time we could agree with them,
To tell the truth,
Was when it's time to go
To the voting booth!

Should I mention this?
Is it even fair?
When I say some of your friends
Have problems with their hair?

In fact, a few of them
Need a miracle!
So we would take them
To see the Weave Oracle!

Our competition might drop a dime
To tell Po Po of our alleged crime!
If we are victims of some jive bust,
Call Partna and Partna to defend us!

I know that Fine Partna
Has a special way,
Of working with the evidence
Like DNA

While the prosecutors
Might laugh and scoff,
We'll have the last laugh
When we get off!

While our getting together,
I'd love to discuss,
Time for me to get
Honest and serious!
I used to be the master
Of fortune and fame,
1979 was when
I jumped out the game!

Your beauty and talent
Deserve much props,
 But I'm probably old enough
To be your pops!

I no longer drive a Bentley,
A Beemer or a Caddy,
Which means I can't afford
To be your Sugar Daddy!

Despite the fact
That you are so hot,
A broke boyfriend is something
You already got!

The thought of being with you
Is oh so nice,
That's why I still wouldn't mind
Rollin' with dice!

She, or Psycho Babe?

How the heck do you decide,
To choose one lady and let the other one ride?
I ain't sure, but I'm just askin'
This question once posed by John Sebastian.

No disrespect to either female,
While trying to choose my mind did fail!
My brains went from one head to the other,
A fact which did not help this brother!

What's done is done, I should let it be,
But, first, let me tell you about She!

A tisket, a tasket,
She gave me several baskets,
Though I found her desirable
I never really asked it!

When I paid her a compliment,
It backfired and She snapped!
I couldn't have been hurt worse,
If I actually got slapped!

She told me of the stars She knew,
Her tales got me curious,
When I asked her about her past,
She began to get furious!
I wondered 'bout the name She used,

Paul Wilson

Singing back in the day,
But She don't get no royalties,
So that name She won't say!

She would always start to cringe,
When I'd recite my phonics,
Embarrassment envelopes her,
'Cause I be speakin' Ebonics!

Black folks are brothers and sisters,
This threw her in a lurch,
She told me this reminds her,
Of a preacher in a church!

I must admit She has a flair,
For style and design,
She made suggestions for my place,
And I thought that was fine.

When next She came to see me,
She let her disgust show,
But I'm just glad I got this place,
I moved here from Skid Row!

The improvements that She prescribed,
Couldn't happen fast enough,
On General Relief,
I can't afford that fancy stuff!

Livin' in the fast lane's
What caused me to go broke,
Keepin' up with the Joneses,
Getting' up for the down stroke!

For me, the finer things in life
Are gonna have to wait,
The place in which I now reside
I got on Section 8!

Right now, I'm doing good
That I get enough to eat,
The funds I get just cover
My rent, the lights and heat!

But I derailed my train of thought
By talking about me,
Back to the subject at hand,
I meant to discuss—She!

A higher plane of consciousness
Is where She's on her way,
Just when She will arrive there?
At present, I can't say!

This goal She's in pursuit of at
All due deliberate speed
The Pleadian Agenda is
What She wants me to read!

We are under the control,
This fact She did mention,
By beings who exist within
The fourth and fifth dimensions, Hmmm
My favorite Fifth Dimension
Is Ms. Florence LaRue
While others were so much in love
With Marilyn McCoo!
I think She is uneasy

In this American place,
I feel She would be more at home
In European space!

Were it within my power
I'd wave my magic wand,
And send her where She wants to be,
That's back across the pond!

Before She gets her wish
To travel back so far,
I hope those folks in Malibu
Give her back her Guitar!

To She I want to wish a fond
Farewell goodbye wave,
'Cause actually She rescued me
From the clutches of Psycho Babe!

From Psycho Babe, I first sought
Some physical relief,
It seems instead that I received
A massive dose of grief!

The first thing that I noticed
Was that Babe was foxy!
So one Thursday I skipped out
To take her to the Roxy!

I thought that I would go there
To hear her do her thing,
However, what I quickly learned

Was that Babe can't sing!

I'm sure that once upon a time
Babe was great eye candy,
But now that years have passed her by,
A voice would come in handy!

Babe thought I could provide some funds,
And her warmness felt nice,
But when Babe found out I was broke,
Her warmness turned to ice!

It took too long for me to learn
what Babe was all about.
Babe took me straight to Heaven
And then I got kicked out!

While I neither smoke nor drink,
I surely don't do drugs,
I don't enjoy the company
Of unfamiliar thugs.

I be on the up and up
And I like to play fair,
But in Babe's world a guy like that
is nothing but a square!
Babe is nice and friendly
In certain situations,
But her niceness goes "Kapoof,"
Without her medications!

Babe always loses when Babe plays

Her money-grubbing game,
But when it blows up in her face,
All others are to blame!

Returning from the Roxy
I got a text from She,
And suddenly it seems Babe caught
A case of jealousy!

One day when She was visiting
Babe wanted to come in,
But when Babe learned that She was there
Babe became a wet hen!

We are Becoming the Borg!

When I first started doing open mike nights, I ran across this comedian named Jeffrey Baldinger. I talk about him in my Zulu Alpha Rap/Poem. This piece is based upon his routine about Scientists.

Jeff is not impressed by Sir Isaac Newton. Ike was zoned out sitting under a tree when that apple went oops, upside his head! But he gets credit for discovering gravity. Say what? Gravity was already here! He just gave it a name.

I am circumspect of Sir Ike my damn self! He is looked upon as a great mathematician and physicist. Really? In his classic work, *Principia Mathematica,* you have to read past page 200 before he tells you that one plus one equals two!

Jeffrey also talks about the physicist Werner Heisenberg. He is a Nobel Laureste best known for his "Uncertainty Principle." How about that! He gets the Nobel Prize for not being sure!

Actually the uncertainty principle is the reason that transporters on "Star Trek" won't work. In one episode of "Star Trek: the Next Generation," Engineer Geordi La Forge makes reference to the Heisenberg Compensators malfunctioning.

It turns out that Heisenberg was one of those German Rocket Scientists who was brought over to America at the end of World War II as part of "Operation Paper Clip." I don't get it! Why would our government want a German Rocket Scientist who was "uncertain" about his work? Maybe so the Russians wouldn't get him first!

I'm going to start drawing some parallels and similarities that some of you Star Trek fans out there might pick up on. For instance, the United States Navy studied the bridge of the Starship Enterprise when designing the command and control centers of its newer warships. The Navy also has a "Rail Gun," which could be considered a first generation

"Phaser." It is so big that it has to be mounted on a battleship. Who knows, they may already have "Photon Torpedoes!"

The "Communicators" that Captain Kirk and his crew used – you just flip open and start talking. "Beam me up, Scotty!" Or, if you're a Klingon – "Maaltz, Chung Chu!" Think of the designs of some of the cell phones we have today.

And what about Lieutenant Uhura, Kirk's communications officer and occasional love interest? Boy, was I jealous of Kirk. He got to be the "Space Cowboy" and the gangster of love at the same time! I actually paid little attention to Uhura until:

a) I learned that her name was the Anglo-feminized version of the Kiswahili word "Uhuru," which means "Freedom."

b) Lt. Uhura wore that 2-piece Starfleet uniform, a virtual "Space Bikini." I think I was fourteen years old when I first saw that episode. I had to roll my tongue back up in my head! I am certain she inspired at least two generations of geeks and nerds of varying races, creeds, genders, and preferences, but understandably, I digress.

That device that Uhura stuck in her ear when contacting Starfleet headquarters via the subspace frequency! Think about it– that's Bluetooth! I wanted to stick my tongue in the Lieutenant's ear and try a hailing frequency of my own. Oops! There I go again. Has anybody figured out that I had a serious crush on Nichelle Nichols?

There are many movies, television shows and cartoons which foretold our future. For those of you asking, "Where's my Flying Car?" Look around they're all over the place! You just need a grip of money and a pilot's license to drive one!I'm sure some of you have figured out that I'm now gonna talk about the pioneering cartoon of the 1960s, *The Jetsons*. Drive to Los Angeles International Airport (LAX). As you roll past terminal one, look to your left. You will see the theme building, also known as, "The Spider."

It looks just like the Skypad Apartments, home of George Jetson, his boy, Elroy, daughter, Judy, Jane his wife, dog Astro and Rosie the robot maid. In one episode, Elroy is approached by a T.V. Producer, who want him to star as "Space boy." While the producer is making his pitch, you see and hear something beep on Elroy's hip.

Elroy says, "That's just my mom, calling me on my 'Frequently.'" Pull out your cell phone and hold it up. This is a "Frequently!"

In one of those '60s spy movies, "The President's analyst," the late actor/comedian Godfrey Cambridge talks about "TPC" (The Phone Company) implanting microchips in people's brains. This would enable people to communicate with anyone similarly equipped just by thinking about them.

We have become so attached to our iPods, iPhones, Androids, Blackberries, Laptops, Notebooks, etc., that I fear we are slowly insidiously becoming, "The Borg." You just knew I was gonna come back to "Star Trek" again!

The Borg is short for "Cyborg," which itself is short for "Cybernetic Organism." They travel around in cube-shaped spacecraft assimilating planets and cultures alien to them and their technology. Their motto is "Resistance is Futile."

They came from the Delta Quadrant of the Milky Way Galaxy. According to Star Trek lore, Starfleet has only explored 11% of our galaxy, primarily in the Alpha Quadrant.

Captain Picard and his crew are thrown into contact with the Borg by "Q," a near god-like entity who gets his or its jollies by meddling in the affairs of any species capable of interstellar travel.

Black Writers on Tour 2013

Choosing between two events is a good thing,
Makes you set your priorities in swing,
Black women's health is as important as any other
A different focus was sought by this brother.

Our local station even offered us a man cave,
which was fine for any other Bill or Dave,
But I cater to a different plan
'Cause I do not profess to be a cave man!

The last Saturday in April I chose not to enter
the Los Angeles Convention Center.
Instead, I took that long bus ride
to Carson, to lengthen my mental stride.

Why did I go there? I'll tell you what for!
To check out Dr. Rosie's
Black Writers on Tour!

For the Elders, the youth and the in between,
There were workshops pertaining to every scene.
If you think you should write a book,
You could meet some published authors—take a look.

There were vendors there of every kind
You could sample new products and expand your mind.
Bring your children to this special place
They can get a head start in the knowledge race.

Let their mental roots
Spread like a tree trunk,
Learn to solve mysteries
With Detective Skunk!
If a search for action
Is your plan,
Get ready for adventure
With Danger Man!

Do you have a story
You think is groovy?
Learn how to make your book
Into a movie!

Get to know the secrets
Of the publishing game,
Self-promote your book
And increase your fame!

Everybody has a
Story to tell.
At Black Writers on Tour
Learn to do it well!

Black Writers on Tour – Poetry Jam

Thought I would come and walk away
With the grand prize for what I have to say,
Been comin to BWOT for years,
Only been writin'& rhymin' for one,
Some of these poets might make me their son!

Never paid attention to poets 'til I became one
Don't know the difference between
Rhyming couplets and iambic pentameters
Don't know how to set up poetic parameters

Tried researchin' cognitive dissonance,
Gotta learn about assonance and consonance,
Maybe then I can develop some resonance,
And try studying some poets in residence.

Been attending open mike nights lately,
They fed my ego and I ate it up greatly,
Had me believin' that I was deep,
But when it comes to rhyme capital I'm sorta cheap!

Don't get me wrong, I got something to say
Expressing poetry, there's more than one way.
Some folks would start off and seem to ramble,
Found out that's just called preamble!

Those kind of poems begin sounding disjointed,
Then get pulled together becoming well-appointed,
I'm gonna have to sit here and think awhile
And figure out if I even have a style!

Paula Who?

Who cares about Paula Deen,
The southern TV cooking queen?
It would mean I had no brains
To mainline butter to my veins!

Racial disrespect, you see,
Is normal for her family,
You can tell by what spews from her mouth
She pines for the antebellum south!

Some think her recipes are fine,
But I used to weigh three-hundred nine!
I don't wish to repeat my fall
Giving in to cholesterol!

To wax nostalgic ain't so bad
But channeling slavery makes me mad!

More Material About The N-Word

Ninja? Is the new N-word! Do you remember Sly & The Family Stone. White folks, please take his advice, "Don't call me N-word, White folks." Yeah, young brothers sometimes call me "O.G." I thought that was cool until I figured out they meant "Old Guy!" Perhaps, I'm a wannabe griot, so here's some knowledge I'm gonna drop on you.

Have you been following the 24 hour news cycle lately? If you haven't, and you still think you live in a "Post-Racial Society," you have missed your freakin' wake-up call!

The reason a lot of us older folks don't care for your gratuitous use of the N-word, especially around non-African-Americans, is that you tacitly give non-African-Americans permission to use that word when addressing us.

How do you feel when some White guy who thinks he knows you, says, "What's up, N-word?"

Most likely, you want to beat him down! While he's trying to get away from you, he's saying, "But you guys say it all the time." Here goes some history for you young brothers and sisters who suffer from a terminal case of historical amnesia!

Around the turn of the 20th Century, White racists would attack, shoot, burn, mutilate and/or hang black men (and women) in public, they would invite their women and children to these outings. They called these outings "Picnics." When a crime would occur in some of these small southern towns, the Klan would pick some black guy to hang, whether he committed the crime or not! Think about it – "Picnic" means "Pick a N-word!" Now, do you still wonder why I cop an attitude when I hear you call each other that! Especially around White folks!

June 18, two zero one three, Game #6 to Miami, the Spurs gave a hundred percent, you see, but Miami gave it a hundred and three.

LeBron and Wade ain't finished yet; if they turn up the Heat, there might be an upset!

Does Dominique care about who will win it? No way, 'Cause the Lakers ain't in it! Happy Juneteenth, Y'all!

> Judge Ross didn't like what I had to say
> So he banished me for thirty days
> Why you want to hold a grudge?
> Don't sound impartial to me, Judge!

> Legally, he's been around the block
> Gave props to his frat brother, Mark Whitlock
> Judge went to Morehouse, I've heard such,
> You can tell a Morehouse man, but you
> Can't tell him much!

> Why did I not do the do,
> And go to an HBCU?
> Had I known about the Airmen, G,
> I would have gone to Tuskegee!

What, Me Old?

Went to the Café Industry,
Can't get enough of Queen Sister G!
Ate a nice meal, paid tuition price,
But my rhymes will have to be more concise!

What woke me up to my new quest?
Were the words of the evening's featured guest.
Sought permission from an Elder, golly gee!
I look around, but everyone's lookin' at me!

Guess I need to check the score,
I am not nineteen anymore!

Queen Gia's hot, she ain't no dud.
She compared Zimmerman to Elmer Fudd,
But Trayvon wasn't no Wabbit see
That sick Boy George was wascally!

For a bag of *Skittles*, young Martin got smoked?
Boy George's huntin license needs to
Be revoked!
Dispatch at 911, said, "STOP"
But Boy George is a wannabe cop!
Zim Zim's whacked, bent on destruction
That's why he ignored his instructions!

A Florida jury's not twelve, but six!
That makes tampering an easier fix!
If Boy George is acquitted, what a bummer,
Get ready for a long hot Summer!

Trade-Tech Blues

I watch beautiful faces and slammin' physiques
But my purpose here ain't to locate freaks!
I'm a little too old to be actin' a fool,
And that's not the reason I came back to school.

I wanna update my computer skills,
That's a fact,
The clock is steady tickin',
Now's the time to act.

Blew many opportunities in my younger days,
I rolled up all my options and I smoked them away!
'Cause how can I succeed when all I do is play?
The plans for my success is all I need to lay!

The pity party is over—no more "woe is me,"
That isn't gonna take me where I wanna be.
If there's one main rule in this knowledge game,
It should be to stop lookin' for someone to blame!

Excuses and complaints won't do me no good,
Need to jump in the books, like I know I should.
What difference do it make, how the kids are now?
Take a lesson from Bart Simpson, "Man, Don't Have a Cow!"

So what my V.A. money is gonna come late?
Just be happy that it's coming at any damn rate!
When I look back on where I was two years ago,
I've come a long damn way, but I got further to go!

From South Africa to South L.A.

—◦═══◦—

In the spring of 1977 an acting troupe from South Africa came to U.C. Irvine to perform. They specialized in the plays of White South African playwright, Athol Fugard. I believe his current play at the time was, "Sizwe Banzi is Dead."

This acting troupe was brought to America by a Christian organization. This organization also planned their itinerary. "On Monday, you will perform at UCLA, Tuesday, you'll go to Disneyland, Wednesday, USC, Thursday, Knott's Berry Farm." And so on.

Several troupe members began to ask questions. "Since we are in Los Angeles, may we visit Watts?"

"Oh no, you don't want to go to Watts. It's too dangerous there!"

"We are from Soweto. How much more dangerous can Watts be?"

On the day the troupe was to visit Knott's Berry Farm, several of them "Missed" the bus that was to take them there. They went out on to the street, flagged down an RTD (now MTA) bus and asked the driver how to get to Watts. An hour or so later, they were standing in front of the Watts Towers.

The local residents wanted to know who these strange – sounding brothers were and why they were here. When the troupe told the locals they were from South Africa, all of a sudden everything was cool. The troupe was welcomed as fellow freedom fighters. We have Gil Scott-Heron to thank for that.

In 1975, Gil Scott-Heron released the album, "From South Africa to South Carolina." He is responsible for changing a call and response greeting we had back then. It used to go? "What's the Word? Thunderbird!" He changed it to: "What's the Word? Johannesburg!"

Because of Gil Scott-Heron, I learned about the "Dom Book" passport that Black South Africans had to carry in order to travel within their own country! I also learned about the imprisonment of Nelson Mandela. By this time (1975), he had already spent over a decade behind bars.

When the Soweto uprising occurred in 1976, Gil Scott-Heron became a much sought after spokesperson about the troubles Black people were having in South Africa.

Were it not for Gil Scott-Heron, I would never have learned about Karen Silkwood, the Clamshell Alliance, and the problems with nuclear power plants and the waste they produce. The songs, "Barnwell," "We almost lost Detroit," and "Shut Um Down," come to mind.

Long before the movie, "Miss Evers Boys" came out, I knew about the government's Syphilis experiments on Black men, because of "Tuskegee 626."

The piece "Aint No New Thing" talks about how in 1896, brothers created a new style of music, the mainstream culture called "Ass Music." But the ass would not be kicked! It then became known as "Jazz."

The Anglo-American version of slavery deprived enslaved Africans of their drums. But the rhythms remained in our DNA. That's why the Africans said, "Merci Beaucoup": on a racetrack in France.

Conscious rapper Chuck-D of *Pubic Enemy* called rap, "The Black Community's CNN." This is why in "Message to the Messengers," Gil Scott-Heron admonishes young rappers not to act like you know, but to know what you are talking about.

He also encourages them to do their own research and not depend on the mass media to tell them the truth. The line, "Why Would They Tell You?" comes to mind.

I have an album of his called "Minister of Information." Gil Scott-Heron earned that title over and over again!

Remember this line from a Tribe Called Quest, "Industry Rule #4080, Record Company People are Shady! You better watch our back "cause I think they smoke crack. I don't doubt it, look at how they act!" I am almost sure the tribe was influenced by this line.

"Do you really want to be in show business? That instant high and constant come and go business, got you provin' exactly how much you don't know business and people sell their souls wanna be in show business, all right with me."

The revolution does not begin in the streets; it begins in the mind. That is why it will not be televised. Information leads to knowledge. Knowledge is power. Load up! "T-minus war and counting!"

Rules of Engagement for Flight School

The purpose of this particular piece is twofold. First, I wish to maintain a mutually beneficial environment for the patrons of the Industry Café and myself. Second, I need to remember that certain words and phrases are frowned upon here.

There was a time in my life when upon hearing me, you would swear I was the pilot of a B-52! I dropped so many F-Bombs! Over time, however, I came to this realization, I did not put myself through college just so that when I got angry with someone I could call them a stack of Mike Foxtrots!

Oh, that's another thing. My military experience brought me in touch with the phonetic alphabet. This enabled me to express myself in the following manner, when I thought some guy's mother was a dog, I could call them a Sierra Oscar Bravo and leave them scratching their heads as I walked away, snickering under my breath.

This creativity in expressing by outrage first started when I was in high school. I had Mrs. Jones for English and Drama. When she got tired of our antics and horseplay, she would say this at the top of her lungs, "The biggest person in here is me!"

Once the football players realized she was correct in her assessment, even they would sit down and shut up!

Mrs. Jones had us read the play called "Antigone." She forgot to tell us this was a Greek tragedy and that the name wasn't pronounced the way it looked. We called it "Anti-Gone." We asked, "Doesn't that mean you didn't go anywhere?"

It gets worse; "Antigone" is part of a trilogy about a guy named Oedipus. There's "Oedipus Rex" and "Oedipus at Colonus." Oedipus sounds more like a description than a name. He did what? I hope he made her bathe first!

Mrs. Jones tells us that Oedipus is looked upon as a hero because he solved the riddle of the Sphinx. The Sphinx is supposed to jump off his pedestal, onto the road and confront travelers with this question: "What walks on four legs in the morning, two legs in the afternoon and three legs in the evening?"

If you cannot solve the riddle, the Sphinx devours you on the spot! If you do solve it, the Sphinx jumps off the cliff and destroys itself. However, once you leave, the Sphinx pulls itself together, jumps back on its pedestal, and awaits the next victim.

Wait a minute, Mrs. Jones. I thought the Sphinx was in Egypt. What are the Greeks doing there? Sidebar: Read *Stolen Legacy* by George G.M. James. Maybe that will explain it.

O.K., back to Oedipus. The trilogy is a tragedy because Oedipus kills his father and marries his mother.

"Mrs. Jones, that makes Oedipus an O.G."

"What do you mean by that, young man?"

"Well, if Oedipus' father was anything like my dad, he would need at least an army or two to do that, and if he then married his mother, doesn't that at least make Oedipus the original Mike Foxtrot?"

Mrs. Jones had no idea what she started by having us read that play. I would tell people off by saying this: "Ingest mass quantities of bovine fecal matter and expire you Oedipus, you!"

Oh, by the way, the answer to the riddle of the Sphinx is man. As a baby, he crawls on all fours, as an adult he walks upright on two legs, as an old man he uses a cane. I guess that was before they invented crutches.

⟶

The first time I heard your father on the radio, I was a freshman in college. The White boys on the campus radio station played, "The Revolution Will Not Be Televised." I thought, *Who is that, the Last Poets, or the Watts Prophets?* When I learned it was neither, I had to find out who this Gil Scott-Heron brother was.

Being a poor, starving student means I wasn't always able to afford the albums that I most desperately wanted. This makes sense because

I also couldn't afford a stereo to play them on. When I purchased my first CD player boom box, I set out to collect as many Gil Scott-Heron CDs as I could find. He once described himself as a Bluesologist. I was attempting to become a Gil Scott-Heronologist.

He sings about how Billie Holiday and John Coltrane can help wash your troubles away. Gil Scott-Heron was responsible for helping me maintain my sanity!

I only started performing at open mike venues in May of 2012. When I heard that you hosted one, I had to come here to check you out.

When I first saw you, I wanted to say, "Excuse me, young lady. Is your mommy the host here?" I was pleasantly surprised when I learned that you were the person I sought. You could definitely win my contest for spokes model!

While I wouldn't say you are itty-bitty, you are a skinny Minnie. This is where people could get confused about you just by looking at you. You told the audience you work at UCLA. People there think you are a student.

Though you possess the looks of a stylish hairdresser, once I heard you speak, I took you for a lecturing professor!

At Industry Café/Natural High/Flight School, I've heard you referred to as, "The Queen." I concur that you are of spoken word royalty, therefore, I pledge to you my spoken word, loyalty.

Yes, you are a queen, but you look like a princess, and you're on your way to becoming an Empress!

Your costume was that of an angelic dress, ooh! I am now confused as just how to address you.

The normal thing to say would be "Your Highness," but I very much want to call you "Your Fineness!"

I know that your words are meant to inspire, but hearing you say them just sets me on fire!

No need to apologize when reporting a crime; keep uplifting the righteous and exposing the slime.

It's clear that you've taken your father's advice. You can drop hard facts while still being nice.

A line from your father explains this just so. I'm acting like you didn't already know.

"Four letter words and four syllable words will not make you a poet. It will only magnify how shallow you are and let everybody know it!"

You dressed as an angel with wings and a halo, you want us to stand up and act: Not just lay low!

I voted early, you thought that was dandy, so you offered me two pieces of candy! Coming from you now that was all good; I like the idea of chocolate angel food!

All Hail the Queen!

I had to leave early, but wanted to stay,
As some of my new friends had come out to play.
To hang out and hear them, that would have been great
Lady Basco, Cassandra and D.J. Real 8!

Do they change their words, I know that I do,
Using expletives at your place is taboo!
I'd follow you to the East, the West, or;
When you hold court, I'd be your Jester!
I know that I would not be a fool.
If I were to matriculate through your school.

From you and from others, I gained
More knowledge
Than from all of the years that I
Spent in college!

I'm glad I discovered your spoken
Word scene:
That's why I wrote this piece—
All Hail the Queen!

Observing GIA Scott-Heron's "HOT"

Check yourself while you're still able,
Always read the warning label,
It's there for a reason, Mister,
Caution approaching, Queen Sister!

She will warn you that she's hot,
Is she boasting? I think not!
Sister states a natural fact,
Brother, how you gonna act?

Compared to her verbal style,
My rhymes seem quite infantile!
I will have to risk the burn,
From Queen Sister I can learn.

Just because she is so fine,
Don't mean that she lacks a spine.
While she's getting to the point
Sister also rocks the joint!

Like a moth in search of light,
I roam through the moonlit night.
Leaving ignorance behind,
I seek to enhance my mind.

Other directions I did test
Now I think I will try west.

Aimless? No! For me don't pity,
As I head for Culver City.

Heard from people in the know
That this is where I should go.
To hear what they have to say
At the Industry Café.

Now I must admit that I
Was searching for a natural high,
Got there during a re-tool
Now they call this place Flight School.

Immaturity was showing;
Answer's here I'm still not knowin'!
But I need not wonder why
They will show me how to fly!

Take a seat and hear the mission
Yes, you have to pay tuition!
Learn the lesson, pass the test,
Get back more than you invest!

I think you will like it here,
Such a friendly atmosphere.
Helpful faculty and staff
Assist you, sifting through the chaff

Three instructors you will see
O. Smith, Queen Gia and Hank G.
With back-up from their house band
form a synergy that's grand!
I sat down at the front table,

Did not heed the warning label.
Suddenly I'm drippin' sweat,
Her fineness is on the set!

Aimed her anti-aircraft Gatts
At Willard and his flying rats,
Put them on blast, called out their names
And sent those vultures down in flames!

Told Sarah Palin, more lame than Urkel
Take her teabags back to the Arctic Circle
On his next move, please take note
Queen encouraged us to vote!

This fact should not be neglected
Obama got re-elected!
Conservatives are dazed and dizzy
Time now to get really busy!

Remain fluid, don't be stiff
Prepare for this "Fiscal Cliff"
Republicans are hatching schemes
To forestall progressive dreams.

Stand up with the Sister Queen,
Vigilant and on the scene,
Enemy is in retreat
Queen Sister Gia brought the heat!

9 April 2013

⇥

From: Paul V. Wilson
       AKA – Joe Average Brother
       A Legend in My Own Mind!

To: Your Fine-Ness,
       Queen Sister
       Gia Scott-Heron
       Daughter of the Minister of Information
       Granddaughter of the Black Arrow
       Principal Instructor: Flight School

Care of: Industry Café, Culver City

Re: Unplanned Leave of Absence

Dear Queen Sister,

Please forgive and excuse my unplanned leave of absence from your Flight School. This was due to what the Homeboy's Shopping Network might refer to as a Blue Light Special – "We're Changing' Locations!" While this move was anticipated, it had to be executed rather abruptly. The good news is that I have successfully escaped Skid Row and am now in possession of my own hanger/workshop (apartment).

I regret having only attended one class in January. I wanted to recite an essay I wrote on the Reverend Doctor Martin Luther King, Jr.

Missing all of February prevented me from performing my series concerning Black History Month. You once introduced me as a historian. Wow, what a rush! Three things that I enjoy about Flight School are as follows:

1) The cuisine at Industry Café
2) The Eye Candy
3) The Ego Munchies: Yum, yum, yum!

I wanted to be there in March to help you celebrate your birthday. I assumed it was in March because of something you said about not being happy with you and Willard (Mitt Romney) both being Pisces. My brother is Pisces, his birthday being February 25th, but as your father states in the Ghetto Code, "There is Something Wrong with February."

I really wanted to be there to observe your father's birthday, as I have several pieces concerning him. His music, his poems and his commentary are probably more relevant now than when he wrote and performed them.

For example, think about former LAPD Officer Christopher Dorner. Regardless of what people think of him, I am reminded of Mark Essex. Gil Scott-Heron's version of "Inner City Blues" talks about the panic Mark created in New Orleans in January of 1973.

Both Mark Essex and Christopher Dorner were ex-Navy. They both killed or wounded several police officers. Based on what they did, you basically knew they weren't gonna make it to a court room in one piece! Both were terminated with extreme prejudice.

I now reside on 11th Avenue, just south of Jefferson Blvd., in L.A. On the southeast corner.

Of that intersection is a mural depicting various scenes from the Civil Rights and Black Power Movements.

Considering all the mass shootings which have occurred in the past year, almost too numerous to mention, Gil Scott-Heron is accurate in his song, "Gun," "This is a Violent Civilization, if Civilization is Where I am… The Philosophy seems to be, Least as near as I can see, If Other Folks Give Up Theirs, I'll Give Up Mine."

I shall attempt to improve on my attendance in the future.

Yours truly,

Joe Average Brother

P.S. In the movie, "Blackwax," Gil Scott-Heron is walking down the street near the White House with a "Cute little chocolate girl." At times, she appears to be leading him. Is that you? If so, he was just preparing you for the leadership role that you presently occupy.

PVW/JAB

Queen Sister Gia's Flight School

If you're tired of the sound
You make being down here on the ground,
When you seek spoken word fun
Tuesdays, go West on Washington

You can display your brand of witty
At Industry Café in Culver City.
On open mike night, it would be so cool
Were you to enroll in our Flight School.

They used to call this place Natural High
And when they changed the name, I wondered why?
While pondering that particular mystery,
I researched Black Aviation History

There are many Black flyers whose glory they share
With astronauts Bluford, Gregory and McNair.
Over "The Nam," flying mission quite scary,
Were brothers like Chappie James and Fred Cherry.
They shot Cherry down; he spent some hard times
In the Hanoi Hilton accused of war crimes

Back in Korea, some brothers took flight,
Like Marine Frank Petersen, the O.G. Black Knight,
The fighter in which he took to the air,
Was that big honkin' gull-winged F-4U Corsair

Paul Wilson

The fastest of prop jobs, it would not win bets
When racing against those MIG-15 Jets
But prevail he did, his career took him far
By the time he retired, he earned his third star!

There were four squadrons of brothers who,
Protected those bombers in World War II
Sit the young ones down, they'll say "Golly Gee"
When they learn of the Airmen of Tuskegee!

Our government actually tried to prove
When it came to flying, brothers couldn't move,
But they were so well-trained and thoroughly tested,
From the White Bomber Pilots, their escort was requested!

Before the Red Tails were flying their sorties,
There were Black Flying Clubs in the 1930s!
This one Black pilot goes back even more
To the days just after the First World War.
This pioneer was no daring mister,
In fact, this pilot was a sister!

Bessie Coleman, remember the name,
As she is the lady of barnstorming fame
In 1921, a prejudiced stance
Forced her to seek her pilot's license in France

In the late 1980s, I happened to spy
A one-woman play called, "I'm Gonna Fly."
Ms. Sonia Jackson told the story
Of Bessie Coleman's rise to glory!

Did you learn this in school? Now hear this, son,
There was a Black fighter pilot in World War One!

Joe Average Brother

You'll have to hit those history books hard
To find the name, Eugene "Jacques" Bullard!
An American brother, he fought not in a trench,
The Yanks wouldn't have him; he flew for the French!

Even if there ain't no such thing as Superman,
That don't stop me from working my plan,
Ain't no reason to act like we are feeble,
'Cause when we work together, we are super people!

Sometimes I think it sounds insane
When Dominique says, "Time to Land the Plane!"
As it applies to this particular set,
Her words are somewhat appropriate!

The mission statement at this Flight School
Keeps you from running out of fuel!
We expand your mind and enhance your brain
So the proper flight level you can maintain!

"Each One, Teach One," you will learn
So nobody will crash and burn!
My question was answered, mama mia!
Thank you your fine-ness, Queen Sister Gia!

So when you hear the sound
From way down here on the ground
It's only me flapping my wings
"Cause I'm Gonna Fly!

Much props and mad respect go out to: Lou Rawls, Grant Green,
Randy Crawford, and a Tribe Called Quest.

Stand Your Ground?

First, driving while Black,
Then, flying while Black,
Now, walking with *Skittles*,
What's up with that?

The way the Zimmerman verdict went
Sets a scary precedent!
Neighborhood watch thinks you're a crook,
'Cause they don't like the way you look?

While Zimmerman did call the cops,
Why did he pull out all the stops?
Had Zim Zim stayed in his damn car,
We would not be where we all are!

Trayvon dead, Boy George on trial,
Black folks trippin' on the prosecutor's style,
Zim Zim's defense flipped the script,
Made you think Trayvon was the culprit.

Their defense of "Elmer Fudd,"
Drug Trayvon's memory through the mud.
Such a cowardly attack
Upon someone who can't fight back!

While racists cheer at this verdict,
With most Black folks this don't well sit!
Here's my theory, now how this sound?
'Twas young Trayvon who stood his ground!

Trayvon walked to his father's place.
While Boy George profiled Trayvon's pace,
George called Po Po, but ignored their plan
"Cause Zim Zim wanna play macho man!

How good could neighborhood watch be
For this gated Florida community?
Their role should be to observe and report,
Not to hunt down young Black men for sport!

Were Zimmerman's actions done in spite,
Trying to keep his neighborhood White?
Too late! 'Cause Trayvon's dad lives there
Did having Black neighbors give George a scare?
Meanwhile, young Martin's getting paranoid
This creepy stalker he must avoid!
Zim cuts Tray off, gets out of his car,
Right here's where Boy George went too far!

Trayvon had to make a choice
Don't run? Let this creep hear his voice!
"Yo, creep! Just who the bleep you be?
And why the bleep you following' me?"

Boy George displayed no police training,
Decreasing the options he had remaining.
Didn't he understand this fact?
When you step to someone, they will react.

If you step to me, I will come at you!
Like what the bleep else am I supposed to do?
With no back-up, the situation was tense
Trayvon exercised his right of self-defense!

Paul Wilson

Why did Boy George choose that night
To confront Trayvon and start a fight?
Zim Zim would not have found it fun
To play vigilante without his gun!

Boy George is a jive-time chump,
He took lessons, but still couldn't thump!
So when he got in over his head
He pulled his gatt and shot Trayvon dead!

Think about this, when has it not been
Open season on young Black men?
Sanford, Florida, Lakeview Terrace
Or Fruitvale Station
It is par for the course
Throughout the nation!

Zim Zim's defense thinks it's so cool
To beat their chest and act a fool!
You taunt the Black community
While we strategize for unity!

But this time we strive to prevail,
Regardless if George goes to jail!
Just check the facts, this will be found,
Trayvon was a hero, 'cause he stood his ground!

Exorcise the Ghost of Willie Lynch
(Week of Halloween, 2013)

⋆▬◉

On the assumption that you nice people would observe Halloween tonight, I had to show up here despite being in the middle of mid-terms at Trade Tech. Last year, Queen Sister Gia Scott-Heron came here dressed as an angel. I was curious as to what her fine-ness would be wearing this year.

While I don't necessarily observe all Hallow's eve, I thought this would be an appropriate time to address the following issue – we need to exorcise the ghost of Willie Lynch.

It is argued that the speech he gave to Virginia plantation owners in 1712 is actually a hoax. Be that as it may, the plan the letter lays out is the dilemma descendants of Black African slaves have been suffering from for centuries—we don't trust each other.

Willie Lynch claims that his mind control techniques saved him from destroying valuable property—his slaves! By separating his slaves from each other by age, gender, height, skin color, and "job," he ensured that they would automatically mistrust any other slave. This also led to those slaves implicitly trusting anyone White, to include the slave master's children.

Due to this mentality, many planned escapes, slave revolts, and other freedom efforts fell short of their desired goals. This would include (among others), the Harlem Renaissance, Civil Rights and Black Power Movements. Some "need to grows." Just gottta tell massa what we's up to!

Unfortunately, some of us believe President Barack Obama's inauguration ushered in the "Posts-Racial Era." As the character, Dap, said in the Spike Lee Joint, "School Daze," Wake Up! We, as a people, have plenty more work left to do.

We, as a people, are still laboring under the ill-effects of the Willie Lynch syndrome. We still don't trust each other, are jealous of anyone's individual success, and won't recognize that success until it receives, "White Validation." As the late Barbara Sizemore once said, "Black people still don't get it." You can look her up on YouTube.

According to Willie the Lynch letter, the effect of his techniques should last for three hundred years. Please check the calendar; it's now 2013. Isn't it time we took control of our own minds?

Due to the policy here at Flight School, I must modify this last thing I want to say. Free your mind, and (guess what) will follow.

I'm Joe Average Brother and I approved this message.

Joe Average Brother's Neighborhood

⋯⊷⊜

23, October, 2012. Welcome to Joe Average Brother's neighborhood. The following is an editorial. The views expressed by Joe Average Brother do not necessarily reflect those of them management and staff of Industry Café and Jazz, or the hosts, content providers and gracious audience of, "Flight School."

This past Saturday, October 20, 2012, was a busy day for many of us. Hopefully, we were flexing our intellectual and political muscles, preparing for this most crucial and important election.

To put it in sports terms, we are looking for a Back-2-Back, we want to see Part 2 of Barack Obama show. We are tired of B-movies, we definitely don't need no freaky-deaky re-rons, especially if this nightmare on Elm Street is going to be starring Willard.

I have seen T-shirts which read, "If James is King, then Kobe must be Emperor." Well, we have to be active members of Barack's winning team, if we want him to continue being President. How can he do the slam dunk if we do not assist?

With the intensity brought on by election season, many of us look for a break. A diversion! Unfortunately, many of us use these diversions as weapons of mass distractions upon ourselves.

For example, a lot of brothers (and others) are fans of impressive mammaries, while forgetting that those lovely representatives do not tell us what is on the owner's mind, or if she has a mind at all!

An event which could be considered "The Bomb" in more ways than one, would be the "Taste of Soul" held on Saturday. "Ground Zero" was Crenshaw Boulevard, from Rodeo Road to Stocker Street.

Don't get me wrong, there were positive events going on at "Taste of Soul." You could get a health screening and you could register to vote, if you hadn't already. You could also try your hand at Recycling Black Dollars, in honor of Mahammad Nasserdeen, peace be upon his name.

With all the sights, sounds and aromas emanating from "Taste of Soul," one could easily succumb to sensory overload and miss out on those things of mutual benefit to the content providers and patrons thereof.

When I heard that Dr. Claud Anderson would be in town on the same day as "Taste of Soul," I knew it was time for me to do a "Midcourse correction." I re-targeted and set my sights for the Carson Community Center.

Dr. Anderson is the author of such books as *Black Labor, White Wealth, Powernomics, and Dirty Little Secrets, Volumes 1 & 2.* While in Carson, I began to wonder if any local people involved in the Reparation Movement were here.

For the past year, I have been out of circulation dealing with medical challenges; I am still trying to figure out who is doing what. I only knew about Dr. Anderson coming to town, because of an ad I heard on *Front Page* two days prior.

There are four community activists whom I know are involved in the Reparations Movement.

One person is Sister Mollie Bell. She is the one who told me about *Front Page* back in the early 1990s. When she calls in, she always begins by saying "Reparations in Memory of our Ancestors."

Then there is Morris Griffin, AKA "Big Money Griff, the Problem Solver." He is currently involved in the campaign to re-elect President Barack Obama.

There's Mary Randall, formerly known as Mary of Paramount. Mary explained the "Doba" standard to me. Doba stands for "Descendants of Black Africans." I like her; she's kinda cute.

Last, but not least is Mr. Peoples. He is the brother who brings the slave ship around to various events in the community. When he calls in to *Front Page*, he always signs off by saying, "There's only two things left; that's the truth and reparations."

I spoke with Mollie Bell and found out that the reparations people were busy this past Saturday. Some were at the "Taste of Soul," getting people to sign a petition concerning reparations. Others were at a reparations meeting in Altadena.

Since I'm getting around a little better now, maybe it's time for me to start attending some of these reparation's meetings <u>and</u> keeping up with what Dr. Claud Anderson is doing. That way, perhaps I can help keep the various organizations informed on what each other is doing. We could either avoid duplicity of effort or attempt to practice operational unity.

Getting involved will keep me from being that guy standing on the sidelines complaining or being a "Monday Morning Quarter Back." As Gil Scott-Heron once said, "No Participation, No Right to Criticize." Hmmm; that sounds familiar. I think I used that in an essay I wrote earlier this year.

I'm Joe Average brother, and I approved this message.

Alicia Randolph – Nice Librarian

Ms. Alicia Randolph is a shining example of why I attend events such as Dr. Rosie Milligan's *Black Writers on Tour (BWOT)*. I have a penchant for intelligent females of the African-American persuasion who smile. Ms. Randolph fits that bill rather nicely!

My first contact with this nice person was on Saturday, April 27th, 2013. I sat in on the BWOT seminar, "Let the Elders Speak." Sister Alicia identified herself as a librarian. Immediately my antennae (among other things) went up!

Look. With what little concern I have for our previous commander-in-chief, at least he gleaned something from his Yale <u>and</u> Harvard "Legacy" education. He hooked up with a librarian. This proves that "W" has at least one redeeming quality!

Sister Alicia spoke about the resources available at the West L.A. Regional Branch of the Los Angeles Public Library. She personally invited BWOT attendees to take advantage of what her branch had to offer.

Since I spend a lot of time at the V.A. Hospital I West L.A., I decided to take Alicia up on her most gracious offer. I believe I made my first visit to that library on Wednesday, May 22nd, 2013. This was almost one month after BWOT.

Ms. Randolph flashed that beautiful smile she possesses when she saw me. She even remembered my name! Which is more than I can say for myself. I had to describe her to the person at the front desk. This task was made easier by the fact that there were only a few African-Americans working at the library.

During my first visit there, I sat down and wrote a poem about BWOT. Sister Alicia invited me to attend one of her "Life Story

Writing" classes so that I could meet with other aspiring writers. She actually read that poem to the class.

This nice librarian also conducts adult computer comfort classes. I definitely plan to attend these classes for several reasons.

1) I presently possess rather limited computer skills

2) I plan to enroll in the Computer Information Systems curriculum at Los Angeles Trade Technical College in the Fall.

3) I get to see my new favorite librarian again!

When I was a student at U.C. Irvine, I had a friend named Ezell Sheppard. He once told me something that didn't make sense to me then, but does now!

"The more you know, the more you realize you <u>don't</u> know!"

Meeting Ms. Alicia Randolph had reminded me of how much fun it is to learn new things and meet new people.

5 July 2013

Well, here I am at my new favorite library. The West Los Angeles Regional Branch. The Los Angeles Public Library is now my favorite, because of my new favorite librarian, Ms. Alicia Randolph. I came here after my appointment at the West L.A., V.A. Hospital, just up the road.

Upon seeing that the next "Wordshop," with author, Hope Anita Smith, would be held the following Friday. I immediately signed up for it. Her encouragement was the ego-munches, which I presently can't seem to get enough of!

The last Wordshop I attended featured two writing exercises which Ms. Smith had us do. One was based on a poem from one of her books. The poem was "Seven Ways to Look at My Father." The assignment was to write about seven ways to describe any particular thing of your choosing. The trick was to do the description in metaphor, not simile.

While I remember paying attention in my Junior High School English class when our teacher explained the difference between metaphor and simile, the teacher, not the subject matter, was the focus of my attention. Miss. Gloria Nolden, who was also my Homeroom teacher and Drama coach was my first major crush. She was the main reason that I never considered playing hooky from school.

Hope Anita Smith explained that when using simile, you employed words "As," or "Like" when describing something. From what I gathered, you use "Is" or "Was" when making a description, using metaphor.

For the second exercise, Ms. Smith wanted us to use a popular fairy tale to explain an event you experienced. I'm sorry, but fairy tales don't seem to do it for me. Perhaps this is because I couldn't connect any fairy tales with anything that was happening in my young life.

I chose to write about Icarus instead. His story reminds me of the life lesson I learned. Not paying attention to the advice offered by my parents, mentors and other elders led to me experiencing unnecessary pain of the physical, mental, spiritual, emotional, and financial varieties. This is why I could relate to the fate that befell Icarus when he chose to ignore his father's instructions.

I immediately became a fan of Ms. Smith when she complimented my "Voice." It took me a while to figure out that she was not talking about my speaking but my writing voice. I have only become serious about writing in the last two years, probably only because my heel injury prevented me from performing my previous occupation, driving.

Since I presently (perhaps fortunately) lack a television, I listen to a lot of National Public Radio and Pacifica Programs. Because of this, I am developing a curiosity about the author Chimamanda Ngozi Adichie. I've heard her being interviewed twice in the past two weeks.

Apparently, her books are extremely popular, as I have had difficulty locating them in the two libraries I now frequent. Both interviews concerned her latest book "Americanah." This is a term used by Nigerians to describe a fellow countryman who has traveled to and lived in the United States long enough to develop American affectations.

Both interviews led me to examine my experience coming in contact with other Africans from throughout the Diaspora. I feel that the American mainstream culture conducts a misinformation campaign concerning Africans and African-Americans. Africans (among others) take their cues and clues about African-Americans from the American media. It seems that if we are not Bill Cosby, Eddie Murphy, Oprah Winfrey, or Barack Obama, we are drug dealers.

In my twenty-three years of transporting people to and from airports in Southern California, I have run across recurring concepts, opinions, attitudes, and patterns concerning African-Americans. The majority of my African passengers, be they White, Black, Asian, or Arab, feel that we know nothing about their continent.

My job, driving for Super Shuttle, was a boring experience. I drove the same freeways, to the same airports every day. I could probably do the job with my eyes closed; however, that is not good for public relations.

Therefore, I would engage my passengers in stimulating conversation. I figured that they either were on their way to somewhere interesting, coming from somewhere interesting, or they did something interesting. If I knew something about their destination or occupation, I could use that as a basis for a stimulating conversation. This would be for the mutual benefit of myself and my passengers. They could get where they wanted to go in one piece, and I could learn more about human nature.

With my African passengers, the first thing I would pick up on was their accent and pattern of speech. I would then ask, "Where are you from?" The reply was usually, "I'm from Africa." At this point, things would get interesting.

"You know Africa is a rather large continent. You could take the continental United States, dump it in Africa three times and still have room left over. Would you care to more specifics?"

The response was usually, "It is a small country. You've probably never heard of it."

"Try me."

They would tell the name of their country. I would tell them, which colonial European power ruled their country, what year they gained their independence and who their first president was.

"How do you know all of that?"

"You can learn anything you want to in this country, you just have to want to learn it."

My interest in Ms. Adichie is due to a lady I met when I started attending Spoken Word events. I eventually began performing at these places. Cassandra (I only know her first name) is a beautiful sister from Nigeria. Her signature piece is called, "I come from a People."

Based on my conversations with various Africans and the interviews with Chimamanda that I heard, I get the impression that Africans don't think of themselves by race, but by ethnicity. They don't think about race or color until they come to America. The United States is a very race-conscious society. The whole (freakin') country is the "Race Card." We seem to be more concerned with "What" you are, as opposed to "Who" you are!

Since I've embarked on this writing journey, I am so glad that I am writing down the thoughts I used to just verbally debate. I'm really learning the power of my voice. What I have to say about the world matters

Seven Ways of Looking at my Family

My father was the anchor that kept us from drifting apart from each other.

My mother was the lighthouse which gave us perspective on where we were as opposed to where we were headed.

My brother's footsteps were and are the milestones I use to pace my journey.

My Aunt Odessa was the foghorn that assured me that I was nearer to my goal than it looked.

My paternal grandmother was the book that let me know what seemed new to me had been done before.

My maternal grandfather was the lens through which life's lessons became clearer.

I am the compass influenced by the various magnets I come in contact with. Sometimes, I spin out of control.

For some strange reason I can't get past the story of Icarus. His father, Daedalus, fashioned a way for them to escape their prison. He showed his son what to do, where to go and what to stay away from. Icarus would have made it had he stayed close to his father. Icarus got "High," figuratively and literally, on his newfound ability to fly.

What melted the wax from my wings was the heat (doubt) generated by those who did not possess my father's wisdom. Here I am doing something, and rather well, I might add, until I listened to those who had never tried anything new. I believed I could not do what I was already doing. When I crashed, my so-called friends told me, "You're no better than we are!"

Perhaps, the moral of this story should be, when you attempt to escape your prison, make sure you don't bring the prison with you!

12 July 2013

Once again, I am in West L.A. I was going to come here anyway to attend the Wordshop conducted by Ms. Hope Anita Smith. I had hoped she was as pretty as her picture indicated she was. It turns out that she is more beautiful in person!

Someone from the library called me two days ago to tell me that the book I requested was now waiting for me to come get it. This was one of four books I want to read by Ms. Chimamanda Ngozi Adichie.

No sooner than I get to page seven in "The Thing Around Your Neck," that I find that a hole has been shot in one of my theories about Africans, in general, and Nigerians, in particular. I thought they weren't color struck like African-Americans are. I'm sure the merchant meant what he said to the lady as a compliment. The merchant talked about the "Honey Fair" skin that the lady and her son possessed. He wanted to know why she had "wasted" it on him instead of giving it to her daughter. I wanted to march right into that scene in that book and knock that guy's teeth out!

I remember reading a book called, "Color Complex." One of the authors of that book was White. Perhaps my prejudice is showing, but I wondered why a White person was needed to help explain why we (African-Americans) trip off our particular shade as opposed to other African-Americans.

Malcolm X once gave a speech about how so-called "Negros" attempted to describe themselves—they would always emphasize what other nationality or ethnicity with which they were mixed. Considering how over the centuries so many people have come to America, you can imagine the myriad of permutations and combinations that exist here. Brother Malcolm's bottom line was that we will describe ourselves as "Anything, but Black!"

When I was in college, I dated a young lady who described herself in a way which she thought was witty. "I'm a little bit of Irish, a little bit of Dutch and a little bit of Negro, but not too much." And she didn't say Negro! I abruptly ended the date by saying, "But not enough for me!" Quite frankly, if I chose my dates by their lack of melanin, there were plenty of females in Orange County, California who possessed far less of it than she did. Quite a few of them actively sought the company of, "The Brothers."

In "Color Complex," the authors talked about how Nigerian men sought women who had Coca Cola figures and Fanta (orange) skin. That parallels a line I've been toying with for a poem.

Hip-Hop's idea of a Hottie, European complexion, African body!

It seems that Willie Lynch not only owned a plantation in the Caribbean, but made numerous incursions into the motherland! Our Diaspora appears to be saturated with the syndrome with which he infected us.

What is really interesting to me is the reaction I get when I discuss such topics with a mixed (Blacks and others) audience. Black folks will pull me off to the side and chastise me for "Airing our Dirty Laundry" in public. My question to them is, "What makes you think that White folks don't already know?"

Until the age of nine, I was a sickly child. All I wanted to do was go to school, not spend time cooped up at home or at Children's Hospital.

When I became immune to all the childhood diseases, I couldn't wait to turn eighteen because I wanted to be an Astronaut. I would ask my teachers how could I go about doing that.

Most of my teachers told me, "You have to go to college, honey." So now I started asking my teachers about this strange thing called "College."

In junior high school, I learned that most astronauts were engineers or scientists. I knew engineers worked with blueprints, so I took drafting classes.

By the time I started taking science classes, I had gained a reputation as a class goof-off. My teachers would try to embarrass me, because I wouldn't participate in class discussions. What they found out the hard way was that I spent lots of time at the Vermont Square Library. I tried to read everything in the 500-600 Sections; 500s were Natural Science, and 600s were the Applied Sciences. My favorite was 629.14. I shut one teacher up when I went to the chalkboard and drew a cross-section of a Turbojet Engine.

Like too many African American male students, I was not given the encouragement and support necessary. And like too many teachers, she had underestimated my gifts.

www.ingramcontent.com/pod-product-compliance
Lightning Source LLC
Chambersburg PA
CBHW022307060426
42446CB00007BA/737